THE STORM:

For Your Good And For His Glory

(2ND EDITION)

LISA J. HAYNES

THE STORM:

For Your Good
And
For His Glory

(2ND EDITION)

Unless otherwise noted, scripture quotations are taken from the HOLY BIBLE, NEW INTERNATIONAL VERSION® and NIV®. © International Bible Society 1973. Used by permission of Zondervan. All rights reserved.

Scriptural quotations noted KJV are from the Holy Bible, King James Version.

© Lisa J. Haynes 2003.

All rights reserved. No part of this publication may be reproduced, stored in any retrieval system, or transmitted in any form by any means — electronic, mechanical, photocopy, recording, or otherwise — without prior written permission of the publisher, except as provided by United States of America copyright law.

Library of Congress Number –2023900696
Cataloging-in-Publication Data
Haynes, Lisa
The Storm: For Your Good and for His Glory
1. Spirituality. 2. Religion.

Printed in the United States of America
Dulles Publishing Company
44715 Prentice Drive #62
Ashburn, Virginia 20146

Take note that the name satan and related names are not capitalized. We choose not to acknowledge him, even to the point of violating grammatical rules.[1]

---

[1] *Can You Stand to Be Blessed,* T.D. Jakes. Treasure House. 1994. p. ii.

Prelude

It's been 20 years since the original publication of this book. People have asked about part two, but I never felt called to write a sequel because the keys to surviving a storm have not changed. The storms have changed. The storms that pounded at the doors of my life 20 years ago are history, and some are a faint memory. New storms have blown through and been conquered. But people are battling storms, and while my storms, new and old, might not be your storms, I want to encourage someone to make it through the storm.

I was talking to my aunt, Eleanor Perryman, who wanted a few books for her friends. She recently read her copy again and said, "I can't loan them mine." I had only a few copies left, and after that conversation with her, the Spirit moved me to publish this second edition.

I pray this book might continue to encourage and bless those headed into a storm, struggling through a storm, or headed out of a storm.

Acknowledgments

To the author and finisher of my faith, my Lord and Savior Jesus Christ, without whom nothing is possible: I publicly acknowledge my complete and total dependence upon You. I dedicate this book to You because without You, there is no me. When I thought I would never finish, You continued to remind me that it was not me who was doing the writing. Thank You for trusting me with Your work.

To my husband, my friend, and my soul mate: what the devil meant for evil, God turned it around for good. Thank you for your constant, quiet support throughout this project. I appreciate you because you never interrupted my marriage to my laptop.

To my children, Michael (Anna), Gabrielle, Shekora, Asha, Diandra, Tiffany, Melinda, and Nicole: it is a blessing to be called Mom, Ma, Mum, and Mommala.

To my mother, Bernice Payne: words cannot express my gratitude for believing Proverbs 22:6 – "train up a child in the way he should go: and when he is old, he will not depart from it" (KJV). You invested a lot in me, and this work is part of the return on your investment.

To my memory of my father, Eustace Payne, Sr., who was and still is the toughest man I know. You taught me the value of working hard. I dedicate this to you, Dad. You endured many storms before you got your wings.

To my brother Eustace Jr. and my sisters Carla, Renee, and Terri: thank you for always being in my corner. I am thankful for a family like you.

To my ace Karen (my sister from the Holy Mister): you read the introduction of the original book and said, "keep writing."

To my Godmother, Evangelist E. Lorraine Langham: you are truly a gift from God. He knew what I needed and when I needed it, and at the right time, He sent you. Thank you for walking with me during the dark times.

In honor of My Forever Pastor and father-in-law, the late Rev. Dr. Michael E. Haynes: thank you for a home church that provided the biblical foundation I needed to carry out His will.

Introduction

So, you're in the middle of a storm. The storm is emotional. All around you, the world continues to operate, yet you have difficulty even getting out of bed at times. You dedicate significant time looking for happiness, yet the feeling is temporary. Life seems to be one big burden, but you have it all – so others say. You have a loving family, a nice home, many friends, and a good job (maybe even a good salary). Despite it all, life seems to have very little purpose. You think, "If I were to check out today, would it matter? Let's look at it realistically. The children would have to be raised without one parent, your spouse would have to adjust to a new way of living, your grandchildren may never know or may miss the love of a grandparent, and the immediate family would grieve for a period, but the reality is life would go on for everyone." In the long run, only a few people would be significantly affected by your absence.

But wait – you are saved. You know Jesus in the pardon of your sins and have an intimate relationship with the Father; how could life be this way? Of course, you know that you are more than a conqueror (Romans 8:37). You know that you can do all things through Christ who strengthens you (Philippians 4:13, paraphrased). You know God can do exceedingly and abundantly above all you can ask or think (Ephesians 3:20, paraphrased). You are even aware that in His presence, there is fullness of joy, and at His right hand, pleasures forevermore (Psalm. 16:11, paraphrased). So, what is the problem? How can you be so defeated if you are a Christian? How can you feel this way when you know the Master? There must be something wrong with you. Maybe you are not really saved. You've been told, "Read your Bible, pray, seek God's face," but none of this seems to have worked. You listen to Christian music, hoping to find joy and peace, yet it is temporal. Where is God? If He is omnipresent, why don't I feel Him? If He is omniscient, why doesn't He know I need Him?

You are on an emotional roller coaster that does not stop. Who is controlling this ride, and why won't it let you off? Does this all have a purpose, or is this just satan's plan to steal, kill, and destroy?

That is the nature of a storm. Depending on its strength, things may shift and become unsettled. Life can go from stable and almost boring to being like a ship tossed by a hurricane. However, the one who controls the storm is the key to making it through. This book is for those who cannot see the end of the storm and, as a matter of fact, have difficulty seeing the end of the day. If you have ever been told, "There is light at the end of the tunnel" or "God will deliver you soon" and wanted to scream, this book is for you!

There is no easy formula for surviving a storm, and this book will not reveal a sure-fire solution. It is how you choose to weather the storm that determines if it will be for your good – will it make you or break you? The Rev. Jackie McCullough, on her CD "This is for You Lord," says, "This is not designed to kill you; it's designed to make you better."[2] But, for the storm to make you better, you must not allow it to control you.

---

[2] Rev. Jackie McCullough, "This is for You Lord". Gospo Centric Records, 1999.

Table of Contents

Prelude v
Acknowledgments vii
Introduction ix

Chapter 1: The Storm Is Here 1
Chapter 2: It's Not My Storm 9
Chapter 3: I'm Drowning 17
Chapter 4: Be Careful of the Lifeguard 25
Chapter 5: Broken to Be Made Whole 43
Chapter 6: Hearing God in the Storm 55
Chapter 7: Crazy Trust 69
Chapter 8: Deliverance May Come Inside First 85
Chapter 9: And It Can Get Worse 95
Chapter 10: It's All for His Glory 101

Bonus Chapters

Chapter 11: Illness Can Take You by Storm 115
Chapter 12: Loss and Grief – The Longest Storm Ever 123

Chapter 1

The Storm Is Here

Your life seems relatively normal. You go to work or school and return home. You are involved in the church, maybe a few activities related to your children, and possibly you spend time with a small group of friends. While your life is nothing overly exciting, it certainly would not be described as excessively boring. There could be more to life than what you are experiencing, but your life is not awful or unbearable; it is probably just mediocre. Then one day, everything changes. Your normal, stable life is turned upside down by a storm. What is this storm? It differs for everyone. For some, it might be illness (your own or that of a family member); for others, it might be losing your job, the death of a loved one, financial difficulty, or problems with your children. Whatever form the storm takes, there is no doubt or question when it arrives.

There are different degrees of storms that come into one's life. Some storms are like a rainstorm: they begin quickly and end quickly. Then there is the hurricane with strong winds, lightning, and thunder that can last for hours. And finally, there is the tornado that whips with excessive winds wreaking havoc on anything in its path. It may last for just a moment, but it feels like forever.

Like the weather storm, there are signs when a life storm is on the way. God often sends signs that there is a storm brewing. The adage "the calm before the storm" quite often rings true. I am not saying that anytime there is calm, a storm is brewing, but the scriptures say that satan flees only for a while. The enemy is determined to steal, kill, and destroy (John 10:10). With that as his goal, he sets up plan after plan to destroy us. When he leaves us alone, it is only for a short time, and then he returns. Each time he returns, it is with the same goal: to steal, kill, and destroy. Make no mistake about it-- satan is not interested in playing with you. For those playing with him, rest assured that you will get burned.

It is important to know who or what is causing the storm. There are several causes of storms in our lives:

1. Those that are the result of our disobedient behavior or sin (you are causing the storm)
2. Those that are designed by satan to destroy us (satan is causing the storm)
3. Those designed by or allowed by God to purify us.

The Disobedient Storm

The first storm is personified in the story of Jonah. Jonah was willfully disobedient to God. God told Jonah to go to Nineveh and preach the message of salvation (Jonah 1:1). Some in the theological world take the position that Jonah did not want to see the people of Nineveh saved, which is why he went to Joppa. Once in Joppa, Jonah boarded a ship to Tarshish. Dr. Charles Swindoll describes the background of the issue very well:

"Nineveh was a place of imposing military might. It was the place where the enemy resided. It was the heart and center of the nation of Assyria, a sleeping giant that would eventually sweep down on Israel and annihilate her. Jonah's clear call from God was to travel 500 miles east and bring God's message of repentance to the people of Nineveh. And Jonah wanted no part of it."[3]

Jonah was aboard a ship headed to Tarshish, which is in the opposite direction of Nineveh. The ship ran into a storm, and Jonah was the reason for the storm. By drawing lots (like drawing straws), they selected Jonah to be thrown over. As a result of Jonah's willful disobedience, God had him swallowed by a large fish, where he stayed for three days. The story goes on to reveal that not until Jonah repented of his behavior did his storm end. He could not escape the fish by simply crossing his arms and telling God, "No." Jonah had to obey God's command. God allowed Jonah to be released from the fish so he could be obedient and go to Ninevah.

The "Let's See What You're Made of" Storm

The second type of storm is not the result of obedience to God. The devil does not spend much energy trying to destroy those he already has on his side. If your life is always calm and there are very few bumps in your road, consider yourself in danger (spiritually). You are likely already a friend of the enemy, or, at the very least, you pose no threat to him. Matthew 12:30 states, "He that is not with Me, is against Me…" (KJV). The scriptures also state that "anyone who chooses to be a friend of the world becomes an enemy of God" (James 4:4). There is no in-between for God. If you are not on His side, then you are an enemy. So, if

---

[3] The Insights for Living Study Bible; Zondervan Publishing House; Charles Swindoll, editor; 1996, p. 937.

you have declared yourself a friend of God and earnestly try to serve Him with all your heart, mind, and soul, you are a candidate for this type of storm.

First, Peter 5:8 (paraphrased) declares that satan is like a roaring lion seeking whom he may devour. With that in mind, recognize that your enemy is the devil. He is the worst enemy you will ever encounter. He does not fight fair. The devil will use anything and anybody to destroy you. I have listened to people speak of the devil as if he is the schoolyard bully who enjoys picking on people for their lunch money. MISTAKE! This type of thinking underestimates the opponent. The bully enjoys pushing people around, but he wants them to return another day so that he can bully them again. The devil is not interested in pushing you around; he wants to take you out.

Herein we find Job. The scripture says, "This man was blameless and upright; he feared God and shunned evil" (Job 1:1b). If that was the case, and it was, then Job should have been trouble-free. As a righteous man who faithfully and obediently follows God, Job should have been immune to the storms. But there is no such immunity. We see in the first chapter of Job that satan was roaming the earth. He was looking for something to attack. Job was a candidate for two reasons: 1) he was not a part of satan's army and therefore posed a threat, and 2) God offered him up. If you are like me, you read this passage and thought, "Okay, Lord, I thought you were on our side. Why are you offering Job up as satan's guinea pig?" But as we will discover throughout this book, God does what will bring Him glory (Psalm 115:3). So Job endured a horrible storm, not because he was disobedient like Jonah, but because he was obedient. Remember, obedient servants of God are prime targets for satan.

The "You're Not Quite There" Storm

The third type of storm is the one God causes or allows to happen because He needs to purify you. There are often things, people, and even places in our lives that God wants us to give up for Him. It may not even be a particular sin; maybe it is just a hindrance to our spiritual growth or a block to our blessing. As Christians, we tend to give all the things to God that are easy and call that total sacrifice. There is always that one thing that we are unwilling to give up quickly. It may be pride, money, negative acquaintances, addiction to a substance, or addiction to a person (that last one is often the hardest). Whatever God wants from us, He will get. It is up to us how He does it. It can be easy if we simply submit to His request and give up whatever He is asking for, or it can be difficult if we decide that what we are holding on to is too important.

God calls us to complete submission in every area of our lives. Total submission does not always mean we must give up something physically, but whatever it is, we must let it go. Everything in our lives must be under the control of God. For example, God does not want you to give up your children, as in leaving them outside in the street in the name of Jesus (and if anyone suggests that this is of God, walk far away from them). But He does want you to maintain the attitude that they belong to Him, and since they belong to Him, you ought to treat them as if they are God's property. It is all in the attitude. Let's briefly look at the story of Abraham and Isaac in Genesis chapter 22, verse 2. God asked Abraham to take his son Isaac, the son whom God had promised to Abraham, up to the mountain to sacrifice him on the altar:

> *"Then God said, 'Take your son, your only son, Isaac, whom you love, and go to the region of Moriah. Sacrifice him there as a burnt offering on one of the mountains I will tell you about.'"*

I am sure that Abraham's first response was not, "Okay, sure thing, God." I can only imagine that, like many of us, Abraham thought in his mind, "Can you repeat that one for me, Lord?" But whatever his first thoughts were, Abraham headed for the mountain once he understood what God was asking of him. We will talk about Abraham a bit later, but the point I want to make now is that God was looking for the right attitude from Abraham. That's what sacrifice is all about - it's the attitude. When we do not possess the right attitude about a sacrifice God calls us to make, He may send a storm to prune us. My Godmother once told me, "The making process of God is often quite painful." I have a personal testimony of that truth. When God cleans you up to get rid of the dead weight in your life, it will be painful.

Look at what happened to Joseph in Genesis chapters 37 – 50. Joseph is introduced to the scene as a major character. He is one of the youngest sons of Jacob and the most favored of all the brothers. Joseph's brothers hated him, partly because he was their father's favorite, but I believe the other reason was that Joseph was a brat. Genesis 37:2 talks of how Joseph was "a tattle" and told his father what his brothers were doing. In addition, Joseph had the gift of interpreting dreams, and he angered his brothers when he revealed a dream in which his brothers bowed to him. Clearly, Joseph was naïve if he thought his brothers would receive that interpretation kindly. In modern times, Joseph might have been considered a brat and a bit immature. As the story unfolds, Joseph is forced to grow up. The story is worth your reading in full, but in summary, here is Joseph's storm:

- Joseph's brothers plot to kill him, but instead, they sell him into slavery and lead Jacob, their father, to believe he is dead.
- Joseph is sold to the Egyptians and winds up with power and position in Potiphar's house.

- Potiphar's wife tries to seduce Joseph, and when he does not give in, she rips off his robe and falsely accuses him of propositioning her.
- Joseph is placed in jail for something he did not do.
- Joseph spends two years in prison.
- While in prison, Joseph has the opportunity to interpret Pharoah's dreams, which results in him being placed in charge of Pharaoh's palace in preparation for the famine.
- Joseph's brothers are brought before him during the famine to get food for their family, and Joseph recognizes them, but they do not recognize him. He could have punished them for their treatment of him, but he does not. He embraces them.

What can we glean from Joseph's storm? God wanted to use Joseph greatly, but Joseph was not ready for God to use him. He had some baggage that needed to be dropped; he was too immature for God to use effectively. That spirit of tattling had to go. What God allowed Joseph to go through seems cruel from our perspective. He was separated from his family and sold into slavery. This kind of event in one's life could damage self-esteem and self-confidence.

As if that were not enough, Joseph was falsely accused of trying to sleep with the boss' wife. One of the problems with a lie is that it is hard to defend yourself against an accusation when there are no other witnesses besides God and the devil. If I say that you kicked me in the stomach, and I can tell a convincing story with no eyewitnesses, it will be hard for you to defend yourself against me – even with the truth, especially if I can look like I was just kicked. So, Potiphar's wife knew that her husband would believe her by simply holding on to Joseph's cloak as evidence. When Joseph was thrown in jail for something he did not do, he must have asked, "Why, God?" There is no indication that Joseph was disobedient to God in any way, yet God allowed him to be accused and punished for something he did not do.

But it was in prison that God began to move Joseph closer to his destiny. In jail, Joseph began to interpret the dreams of others, and he knew that this was his gift from God. When the time was right, God gave Joseph the opportunity of a lifetime – to interpret the dream of the Pharaoh. The interpretation of this dream catapulted Joseph into a position beyond anything he had imagined. Joseph was put in charge of the Pharaoh's court. He determined when the food would be gathered and how it would be stored as they prepared for the famine. All along, God had a plan. He just needed to prepare Joseph for it. That meant Joseph needed to grow up for the role of a lifetime.

My Storm

Having identified the three types of storms, I can tell you now that my storm was all three wrapped up into one. The interesting thing about this storm is that it was not my storm, or at least not initially. In the next chapter, I'll talk about what happens when the storm is not yours, but you are experiencing all the effects of the storm.

When satan wants to take you out, he has no rules. He will use anything and anybody. Anyone who has experienced satan's games in full effect knows that he will create the best of lies if he thinks someone will believe them. If someone has ever lied on you, you know it can be difficult to disprove a lie. A lie can take on a life of its own because some want to believe the lie. In my storm, someone's lie turned into a storm very quickly, and it affected everything. It was a storm that began quickly and ended slowly, lasting two years. We'll focus on the storm, not the lie.

Chapter 2

≺● ≺● ≺● ≺●

It's Not My Storm

If you are married or have children, siblings, parents, or any relationship, the possibility will always exist that a storm will come into your life because of someone else. God may send or allow a storm that has more than one purpose. The focus of the storm may be on someone else, but your relationship with that person means the storm's winds may blow directly on you. Those winds may be so strong that the storm could be almost as equally yours as theirs.

Let me give you an example: you are the parent of a 17-year-old high school student who, after a night of partying, drinking, and smoking, gets into a car accident with friends. One of the friends dies, and your child is injured badly and may never walk again. Your child is about to enter a storm. The storm includes grieving for the lost friend, the guilt associated with poor choices, and the emotional battle of dealing with the injury. The storm is the result of your child's negligent behavior – simply choosing to live outside the will of God, but as a parent of that 17-year-old, you are about to feel the storm's winds. All those emotions of guilt, anger, resentment, discouragement, fear, pain, etc., are about to become your problem. Every day your teenager wakes up in your house, you will have to deal with whatever they feel that day. You have become a party to "someone else's storm." But whether the storm is yours or someone else's, the pain feels the same.

Look again at the story of Job. Scripture says that Job was a righteous man, and one day while satan was roaming to and fro, God offered His servant Job. During this storm, Job lost his children, livestock, servants, and health. This story is about Job, and the storm belongs to Job. However, we cannot forget that those ten children who were killed also belonged to Job's wife, those lost servants served Job's wife, and she shared the livestock killed. Everything Job lost, his wife lost as well. The loss of ten children is no less painful to a wife than to her husband; some might argue it is more painful since she carried them for nine months. I would imagine that when Job's health started to fail him, his wife had to care for him and deal with his moods, medical and other needs, and discouragement. Job's wife (whose name was never mentioned) directly experienced "someone else's storm."

Whether the reason for the storm is the disobedience of the person at the center, a test to see what a person is made of, or a spring cleaning of some junk in someone's life, when you are experiencing "someone else's storm," you have no control over when it ends. Even if the object of the storm knows exactly why the storm occurred, as a bystander, you cannot force someone into any behavior to change the storm's course. In most cases, God is working directly with or on the object of the storm, and you must stand by and wait for Him to complete His work.

It's in the Attitude

There is a difference in the way you handle a storm that is directly yours versus a storm that you are a party to, and that difference is the focus of this chapter. It is easy to resent the object of the storm as the seas start to swell and the winds start to blow. Job's wife is a prime example of this. As much as she loved her husband, she had experienced more loss than she could humanly take. In the second chapter of Job, verse 9, Job's wife says to him, *"Are you still holding on to your integrity? Curse God and die!"* Many times, Job's wife is looked down upon for this statement. When you take this statement out of context, Job's wife appears spiritually weak. But look at the circumstances. She had lost ten children, all her possessions, and servants. She was broken. Crushed under the weight of the storm, she had endured all she could. The final blow had come, the straw that broke the camel's back. Job's wife wanted the storm to be over. Whatever it took, she wanted the storm to end, not only for her sake but also for the sake of her husband.

For a moment, I want you to put yourself in her shoes. All these events are happening in your life, and you have no idea why. You cannot identify why God allows such awful things to happen to you and your husband. You struggle to understand why all ten of your children are gone, you went from wealthy to poor, and all your servants are dead. Everything you had seems to be gone. I do not know about you, but if I were Job's wife, I think I would have lost my mind. One day you have it all, then you wake up, and there's a full-scale attack on your life. Everything sacred to you is fair game for the attack. You can now understand Job's wife's perspective. She responded in the flesh, and her larger message was, "I have had enough. I cannot take this anymore. I do not understand why any of this is happening, and I want it to end - whatever it takes." I would agree that it may not be the most spiritual response, but it is certainly an honest and gut reaction to an unbelievable turn of events.

Whatever the degree and extent of your storm, you determine your attitude during the storm. When it is "someone else's storm," your attitude is critical. As with Job's wife, your behavior and words directly impact the object of the storm. Had Job's wife been focused on the captain of the ship instead of the storm around the ship, she might have been able to encourage her husband with words of comfort and reassurance. Her words might have been, "Job, I do not understand this. I am in emotional pain because of these circumstances. I know that you are struggling with this whole thing. I feel overwhelmed, but we're in this thing together. The devil and his demons have launched a full-scale attack on our household, but you and I, with God in our corner, can make it through the storm." That sounds like a fairytale statement, but it's the attitude we must have in the storm.

I can identify with Job's wife. When you're in a relatively short storm, keeping your head up and your attitude positive is easier. When the storm seems never to end, you can easily find yourself at the end of your rope. The Bible gives no indication of how long Job's ordeal lasted, but there is a clear inference that it was quite a long storm. Since it was long for Job, it was long for his wife. When the storm is long, you go through various phases: the "why me?" phase, the "where is God?" phase, the "I can't make it through" phase, the "life isn't fair" phase, and the "when will it end?" phase, to name a few.

I can remember feeling what Job's wife felt. After being in the storm for nine or ten months and having endured the adverse effects of the storm, I, like Job's wife, reached that breaking point. I felt as she did; I wanted it all to end; whatever it took, I wanted the storm to end for my family. In my humanity, I told God (yes, told, not asked) that this storm had gone on long enough, and it was time for him to step in and deliver us. Just so you know, that did not work; a year later, the storm was still around. I cannot be sure, but I guess God got a chuckle from my demand.

I did not say anything as direct and harsh as she did, but I can remember questioning my husband one day, and the essence of my communication was that I wanted to be sure there was nothing he was holding back from God that was keeping us in the storm.

IT'S NOT MY STORM

Now that may not be the equivalent of "curse God and die," but it does certainly create an unsettling atmosphere. My intention was not to be accusatory, but my frustration with the storm's longevity was beginning to affect my confidence in God to handle the issue. If the issue was something my husband needed to give to God, there was NOTHING, and I repeat, NOTHING, I could do about it. Since there was nothing I could do about it, my "Job's wife" attitude was certainly not going to help.

One of satan's biggest weapons in the storm is to attack your attitude. He has you if he can make you believe you cannot make it through the storm. And when someone else is the center of the storm, satan convinces you that you cannot make it, and you translate that to the object of the storm. If the object of the storm is your spouse or your child, your attitude can directly impact how that person weathers the storm. I heard a quote during my storm - I am not sure who coined it, but it summed it up very nicely: "God determines what we go through, but we determine how we go through it." The choice is ours. We can use our energy to fight back against the devil using the weapons God has given us, or we can throw ourselves a pity party and spend that energy wallowing around and complaining about our situation.

For the record, choosing to wallow and complain will not shorten the storm; therefore, it is just a waste of good energy. God understands and may even sympathize with our pity party, but He will never join in. He made us and therefore knows our weaknesses. He knows what we can withstand and when the weight is too heavy. His wisdom far surpasses anything we can comprehend, and with that in mind, you can bet He is thinking something like this: "My poor child, once again relying on her strength. If she could think beyond herself, outside her box, she would recognize that all that energy would be better spent in worship, praise, prayer, and service. I've got to show this child how to look up."

The Devil's Attack on Attitude

So how does satan attack our attitude? Simply put, any and every way he can. He will use anything and anybody to steal your joy. When you are in the storm, it does not take much to throw you off kilter. The slightest thing can set you off. Your children having the house dirty when you get home from a long day's work can cause you to lose your religion. The devil will often send demons to the areas of your life the storm is not affecting so that you begin to feel overwhelmed in all areas of your life. He knows that a discouraged spirit will lead to a defeated attitude. If the storm is related to issues or people in your home, you will quickly find problems occurring at work or even at church that are unrelated to your storm but are nonetheless a cause for additional stress.

You must recognize satan's attacks and do everything you can to fight them. Not recognizing when satan is attacking is the equivalent of throwing in the towel. When you cannot identify that a particular event or conversation is an enemy attack, you will likely be wounded by the attack or possibly end up wounding someone else. During the worst times of my storm, I was short-tempered, agitated, impatient, and generally cranky. When I was not sleeping well, my physical exhaustion would only contribute to this chaotic state of life. Without recognizing that satan was launching a side attack on me, I continued like a gerbil on a wheel, running hard and getting nowhere. Charles Swindoll said it best in his commentary in the Living Insights Study Bible. He quotes psychologist Rollo May: "Man is the strangest creature who ever lived; he is the only one who runs faster when he loses his way."[4]

The more satan attacked, the faster I ran - working harder, doing more to find my way out of his path, busy at church, busy at home, just being busy. And then I figured out why I was in disarray – I

---

[4] The Insights for Living Study Bible; Zondervan Publishing House; Charles Swindoll, editor; 1996, p. 936.

was doing the opposite of what I should have been doing. Because I did not see this as an attack from satan, I was not fighting the enemy with the right weapons. I was not fighting at all, and if I was, it was against me. In 2 Corinthians 10:3-4 KJV, the Word of God states, *"though we walk in the flesh, we do not war after the flesh. For the weapons of our warfare are not carnal but mighty through God for the pulling down of strongholds."*

When you know whom you are fighting, you can fight back. Even amid the storm, you must be conscious of when satan is throwing darts. When you feel like you've almost reached the end of your rope, the walls are closing in on you, and you are unsure which way to turn, do not start running like the gerbil on the wheel. Stop, drop, and kneel. The weapons of your warfare are mighty; the NIV version translates that they "have divine power."

In a later chapter, we will discuss in more depth the weapons we can use to fight this spiritual battle, but it is important to recognize three things:

1. It is a battle.
2. satan is the enemy.
3. You can win.

The last one is sometimes easier said than believed. When the storm winds are blowing so hard that you can barely stand up, believing that satan cannot beat you sounds like one of those religious clichés. In the next chapter, we'll examine the realities of where a storm can take you emotionally, spiritually, and physically.

Sometimes in our "religiosity," we pretend that if we act like everything is okay, it will eventually be okay. We are unwilling to admit, "We are not okay." We wear masks so that no one knows when we are emotionally or mentally in a bad place. Somehow, we equate those down times with spiritual weakness or being unchristian. The Bible indicates that Jesus was very solemn, and maybe even a bit down, as He prepared for the cross. And while what we face in no way could compare to what Christ faced on the cross, where He bore the sins of the world, there is comfort in knowing that even the best can get down on occasion. The key phrase here is "on occasion." Our problem is that once we are down, we have difficulty getting back up.

The spiritual battle has a similar philosophy to a boxing match. The referee counts to ten in a boxing match when a fighter goes down before declaring the match over. The longer the fighter takes to get back up, the less likely the fighter will get up. This can also happen during our spiritual battle: the longer we stay down, the harder it will be to get back up - if we get up. During the storm, it is inevitable that you will fall down. How long you stay down is up to you. Remember, your attitude determines your altitude. Those down times can become defining moments in your life, and God must be a major part of the definition.

During a storm, whether it is your storm or not, you can reach a point where you feel like you are spiraling downward. You begin to lose focus on the positive in your life, and you become trapped in satan's deceptive web of doom. Your attitude becomes that of Glum's character from the old television show *Gulliver's Travels*, who proclaimed at every problem, "We're not going to make it." You feel like you are drowning, and that is where satan wants you. Do not let him win!

Chapter 3

I'm Drowning

I've read that drowning is a terrible experience and certainly one I hope never to have. However, many experience mental, emotional, and spiritual drowning daily, and while not resulting in physical death, it can certainly have deadly ramifications.

If you have never experienced this feeling of mental, emotional, or spiritual drowning, consider yourself blessed. In a storm, when everything seems to be falling apart, and there appears to be no end, it is easy to feel like you are drowning.

The Drowning Experience

What is drowning? Drowning is when satan launches an attack on your mind and makes you believe that you cannot, and will not, make it. From the time you awake in the morning, you are focused on the storm raging in your life, the length of time it has been raging, and how unfair life seems to be to you. That feeling of hopelessness that begins to consume you and control you is called "drowning."

Isaiah 26:3 says, *"Thou wilt keep him in perfect peace whose mind is stayed on thee because he trusteth in thee"* (KJV). This scripture was typed out and posted on the wall in my office. I could quote it word for word, but I could not live it out. Sometimes I could not keep my mind on Him. No matter how hard I tried, I could only see the winds blowing and the waves coming up against my ship. I was drowning.

Drowning results in death, and, for many, this becomes an appealing alternative. I imagine if one is drowning in water, that during this horrible experience giving up and dying seems like a better alternative than continuing the struggle to stay alive. So, it is for the victim of mental drowning. The daily struggle to maintain sanity becomes so difficult that giving up becomes a real alternative. Some may never actually consider the act of suicide, but giving up on life and silently hoping for a peaceful end to a difficult life is the softer alternative.

I do not mean to minimize the seriousness of suicidal thoughts and would recommend that anyone considering such an alternative seek professional counseling from their pastor or a Christian counselor. I am not qualified to address this issue, but suicidal thoughts are an enemy attack. Never allow the devil to convince you that you are not a valuable child of God. You are made in the image of God; Genesis 1:27 says, *"So God created man in his own image, in the image of God he created him; male and female he created them."* Now, if God thought enough of you to create you in His image, you know that thoughts of taking one's own life are not of God.

The Devil's Attacks on the Mind

The devil loves to attack the mind because he knows that the mind controls our actions and reactions. When satan can infiltrate your mind, he can throw you off course. Consider this scenario:

someone says, "I need to speak with you when you have a moment." Before you speak to this person, it is amazing how easily you can create two or three different stories of why the person wants to speak with you, how you will react, and who else may be involved. It sometimes amazes me how I can stress myself out about something that has not happened and may never happen, all because I allow my imagination to run wild.

Look back at the story of the end of Joseph's life in Exodus chapter 1. After Joseph's death, his descendants and remaining family stayed in Egypt. Joseph and his generation were dead, but the sons of Israel "were fruitful and increased greatly," according to verse 7. A new Pharaoh came into power who did not know of Joseph or of his loyalty to the previous Pharoah. He determined in his mind that Joseph's descendants were becoming too large in number and might rise against him. Scripture bears no indication that the Israelites had taken any actions that should give the Pharaoh cause for concern. His insecurity and the devil's attacks on his mind resulted in Pharaoh acting based on a scenario in his head. Pharoah's rationale for placing the Israelites in bondage, as documented in the book of Exodus, was based on an imagined, not actual, revolt.

The attack on the mind is more than just an overactive imagination - it is a tool of the devil to rob you of your peace. All of satan's attacks are not large; he is equally as satisfied with several small attacks that accomplish the same goal. Anything God has given you, satan wants to take away. I don't know about you, but for me, peace of mind is a very important element in my daily survival. Without peace, I am anxious about everything; I am irritated by the smallest things and angered by small issues. It's the feeling of a shaken bottle of soda: the feeling that the next issue will cause an explosion. But the Bible speaks to the issue very clearly in Philippians 4:6 & 7 – ***"Do not be anxious about anything, but in everything, by prayer and petition, with thanksgiving, present your requests to God. And the peace of***

God, which transcends all understanding, will guard your hearts and minds in Christ Jesus." The key is to tell Him what is on your mind. Tell Him any way you can. That means forgetting about all the religious-sounding phrases; just talk to Him. Let's digress for one moment and talk about the issue of prayer.

Pray Your Way

If you were raised in the church as I was, you have a very clear outline of how one should pray. You know the right words, the order to use them, and when a prayer sounds good. We focus on how eloquent someone is and evaluate their prayer based on the number of amens and the general reaction of those hearing the prayer. In charismatic worship, the louder the room is during a prayer, the more powerful the prayer feels. Those who enter the church as adults are often drawn into this thinking. Newcomers begin to see prayer as an outward display of rhetorical gifts. Do not be fooled; God is not impressed with our eloquence. When you are desperate, lose the dignity and the need to impress, and just talk to Him. Sometimes you must just look up to your Father and tell Him, "I am having trouble, Lord."

I can remember being in the storm for about ten months and being emotionally at a very low point. I was planning to attend the women's retreat for our church, and I had a few words with God. There was nothing religious about the prayer. My tone and my words might have mortified the old prayer warriors in the church, but it went something like this:

> *Okay, Father, I am going on this retreat because you have made it clear that it is where you want me to be. I could find other things to do with this money, but I will be obedient. Now, I do not mean any disrespect, but if I return home in the same state I left, I will have major issues with you. Right now, I am in no mood for religious*

grandstanding or entertainment. I need more than a good Baptist or Pentecostal sermon or some foot-stomping music; I need an encounter with You. So, this thing is on you, Daddy. I'm doing my part by going - now, You do Your part by making something happen.

And He did just that. I realize that I will not get into any theological seminary with a prayer like that, and the institutional church would frown upon such an unorthodox prayer, but I was not trying to impress anyone. This was between God and me; He knew my heart, and, most importantly, we had a relationship.

There are two points I want to emphasize. First, prayer is a conversation between you and God. If there are other people present, they are only eavesdroppers in your conversation. When you find yourself praying to meet the approval or satisfaction of others, you are missing the boat. In Matthew 6:5-6, Jesus warns the disciples, **"And when you pray, do not be like the hypocrites; for they love to pray standing in the synagogues and on the street corners to be seen by men. I tell you the truth; they have received their reward in full. But when you pray, go into your room, close the door, and pray to your Father who is unseen. Then your Father, who sees what is done in secret, will reward you."** Be sincere in your prayer and forget about the fancy religious talk. I used to tell my teenagers that God understands their language, even when they use slang.

Second, the issue of relationship is important to the way you pray. When you have a close relationship with someone, how you talk with that person is very different from how you would speak to someone you hardly know. The same is true with God. If your relationship with Him is close, you are more comfortable talking with Him informally. If you are following Christ at a distance (like Peter when Jesus went before the high priest in Matthew 26:58), you will not feel comfortable using informal language. God will feel more like a stranger than family.

One final note about the issue of prayer, one of our biggest mistakes in the storm is to stop praying. We can become so overwhelmed by the circumstances of our lives that we do not know what to pray, or we do not desire to pray because of our frustration with God. In either case, the result is the same: we cut off the power source. It is the equivalent of unplugging the refrigerator and wondering why the food is getting warm. We are in the middle of the storm, desperate for strength, and we cut ourselves off from the power source. Humans are considered an intelligent form of life. But this reaction of unplugging from the source sure makes you wonder.

Where Are You, God?

I remember several points in my storm when I felt God was nowhere to be found. I repeated the words that Jesus spoke on the cross, *"My God, my God, why hast thou forsaken me?"* (Matthew 27:46 KJV). Sometimes I felt like I could not make it to the next day. Even more significantly, maybe I did not want to make it to the next day. I was selfishly praying for the rapture. Despite all the wonderful things I had going for me - a successful career, a loving family, a strong church fellowship, and twenty years as a Christian - I wanted to leave it all behind just to get away from the storm. If you have ever felt like you are in a small room, and the walls are closing in on you, then you understand what I mean. I wanted to travel to a remote island, find a cave, and hide.

The storms of life can upset all that seems normal in one's life. A storm can make even a reasonably strong and stable Christian begin to doubt the promises of God. You may wonder, "Am I really saved?" or "Does God love me?" You begin to get angry with God and ask questions like:

- Why me?
- How could a loving God allow this?
- I've been faithful. Where is my blessing?
- What about those who are unfaithful? Why are they not in the storm?

All these questions are the natural result of the shock and pain of the storm. This is particularly the case when the storm is not the result of our sin, the "you're not quite there" storm or the "let's see what you're made of" storm.

You must understand one key in the storm: God is capable of stopping the storm, and He can help us through the storm. He can keep us from drowning all by Himself. However, often we do not or cannot trust Him enough just to allow Him to work, or we do not do what we need to do. As a result, we continue to drown. Because of His grace, God will not allow us to drown when we earnestly seek Him to keep us afloat.

Yet God tries to keep us from drowning, and despite His efforts, we still manage to get in the way. When this happens, He will often send an agent to speak on His behalf. God will send a lifeguard to keep us from drowning. How do you know when God has sent you a lifeguard? As the crowd said in Mark chapter 7, when Jesus opened the ears of the deaf man and caused him to speak, *"He hath done all things well"* (verse 37 KJV). When God does something, He does it well, and there is no question that it is Him. If God sends you a lifeguard or even throws you a life preserver, you must be in tune with Him to know that this is something designed to save your life. Do not make the mistake of not taking the life preserver because you are too busy drowning. I would warn you of one thing: just because people can talk the lingo of a lifeguard does not mean they have what it takes to save your life. Also, just because it makes you feel better in the storm does not make it a life preserver. You must be careful to discern what is and is not from God.

Chapter 4

≁ ≁ ≁ ≁

Be Careful of the Lifeguard

If you have ever taken a lifeguard course to learn to save someone from drowning or have seen a drowning victim being saved, you know that the person drowning is in panic mode. Fearful of dying, the drowning victim searches to grab hold of anything that will prevent drowning. To be a lifeguard requires swimming skills and a degree of strength. As the lifeguard approaches the drowning victim, usually, the victim will immediately grab the lifeguard and cling in desperation. This often results in the lifeguard being submerged underwater for a few seconds. This submersion can be startling even for a moment; therefore, a lifeguard must be prepared. To be a lifeguard, one must possess three characteristics:

- **Mental strength**: Mentally, the lifeguard must have the strength to remain calm while the victim panics and be able to soothe the victim's fears.
- **Physical strength**: Physically, the lifeguard must be able to restrain the victim and, if necessary, carry the victim to safety.
- **Training or knowledge**: The lifeguard must possess enough training or knowledge about lifesaving to

anticipate what might go wrong in saving the victim. The victim, in a panic, might cling so tightly that the lifeguard is too restrained to swim. The lifeguard must be knowledgeable enough to know how to get free without inciting more panic or causing the victim to drown. In an attempt to stay afloat, the victim may unintentionally push the lifeguard underwater. If the lifeguard is not prepared to counter this action, both may drown.

A deficiency in these three characteristics could result in a tragic outcome for the victim, the lifeguard, or both. Spiritual drowning is a similar experience. During a storm, we begin to feel as if we are drowning. The situation and circumstances begin to overwhelm us, and keeping our head above water becomes difficult, if not impossible. We begin to grasp for anything that will keep us from going down. The problem is that we are at risk of grasping the wrong thing in our desperation. Saving a life spiritually requires characteristics similar to saving a life physically, but the most important factor is that God must send the spiritual lifeguard. This is more than someone who attends church or is highly spiritual. When God sends a lifeguard, the person is fully equipped to act as an agent for Him. Let's look at the characteristics of a spiritual lifeguard:

Mental Strength

- Directs you to Christ as the answer to everything.
- Gives advice and shares personal experiences.
- Understands the importance of confidentiality.
- Does not pretend to have the answer to every question.

Physical Strength

- Is willing to invest the time and energy it will take to save you.

Training or knowledge

- Knowledgeable of the Word of God.
- Believes that prayer is a critical part of surviving the storm.
- Does not seek to control you but encourages you to be the person God desires.

My Lifeguard

I have heard it said that a drowning victim going under for the third time is not likely to return to the surface, so a lifeguard must rescue the victim before the third time. God may not work on the lifeguard rule, but He knows when to send the lifeguard. At the peak of my storm, I had reached my breaking point. I held a leadership position in the church, had a preacher for a husband, and had been a Christian for over twenty years, but I was drowning. Every day I felt like I was in a losing battle. I prayed, read books, read the Word, listened to inspirational music, and attended church faithfully, but nothing could stop the drowning feeling.

When I cried out to God with everything I had and asked Him to relieve me of this feeling of drowning, He sent my lifeguard. The lifeguard saved me from drowning and began teaching me to swim. Having a lifeguard appear in your life does not necessarily guarantee you will not drown. The lifeguard must actively do something to save you. God sent a lifeguard who began to pour the Word of God into me in small doses. When the drowning feeling returned, my lifeguard would simply reach out a hand and gently remind me to swim.

The Focus of the Lifeguard

The key element to knowing whether God sent a real lifeguard is to find out where the lifeguard focuses attention. As a teenager, one of the things I found funny was laughing at how curious other people could be. We used to play a joke when waiting for the bus or train by looking up at the sky or ceiling, and someone might even point upward. Then we would watch how many people would look up to see where we were looking. You would be amazed at how curious people are. People would often look for two or three minutes, twisting their heads to identify the mystery.

That is what the lifeguard should do. The lifeguard should be pointing upward to indicate the direction all attention should be focused. You should be like those nosy people, twisting your head to figure out where the lifeguard is pointing. When God sent my lifeguard, I knew it was from Him because the lifeguard always pointed and looked upward for the answer to everything. I never questioned whether my lifeguard's opinion would contradict what God was saying because her advice was always rooted in the Word of God.

The teaching part was critical because I was destined to begin drowning again without knowing how to stay afloat. I had to be taught to speak my mind and rebuke the thoughts of apathy, discouragement, depression, and disillusionment. I had to learn how to find peace in the presence of the Lord. Being in the presence of the Lord did not mean praying for five minutes and running off to the next task but making the time to sit quietly before God (and I emphasize making the time). I had to tell God what was happening inside and then listen for that still, small voice in the silence.

I had to learn the importance of taking the focus off myself, which perpetuates depression and drowning and turning my focus on God. I had to learn to be radical in my personal time with God.

Again, for someone who needs to hear it, constant focus on oneself only perpetuates the feelings of depression and drowning; in the construction world, they call this implosion. I always tell people that if they want to take the focus off themselves and their situation, work with teenagers. They will never focus on you because they are inherently selfish and spend most of their energy on what is affecting them at any given moment.

Staying Afloat

It is key to understand that staying afloat requires action. When you're in danger of drowning, you have two choices: sink or swim. Sinking is easy; it requires no effort or energy. By simply remaining in the water and doing nothing, you will sink. One of the first things many of us learned when we began swimming was the dog paddle. This entails a feverish paddling motion with the arms and hands and what would appear to be a running motion with the legs and feet. While the dog paddle will keep you afloat for a short period of time, it is not the most efficient or effective means of staying afloat - the frantic nature of the dog paddle results in fatigue. It is difficult to maintain this pace for an extended period. A second way to keep from sinking is the "dead man's float." It does not require much effort but entails positioning your body so that it simply floats on the water as if you were dead. If done correctly, the dead man's float may keep you on top of the water for a significant amount of time, allowing you to conserve energy and take periodic breaths. The problem with the dead man's float is that you will move in whatever direction the waves carry you. You will have no control over your direction. A third option for staying afloat is the freestyle stroke. The freestyle involves systematically using your hands and feet to swim forward. By swimming, you accomplish two things: 1) staying afloat and 2) moving in your desired direction. It requires no action to sink; however, our goal should not be merely staying afloat but growing spiritually and making it through the storm – by swimming.

Spiritual Dog Paddle

From a spiritual perspective, we can look at the same options. Using the analogy described above, we can elect to dog paddle. For many of us, the dog paddle entails constantly laboring at work, church, or both to avoid even thinking about the storm or our drowning. We leave early for work and return home late. We volunteer for anything and everything at church as if excessively serving will provide an answer or keep us from drowning. We attend every event possible at church, searching for an answer and looking for the Spirit of God, but we fail to realize that we have not sought God in all our constant movement. We seek substitutes for God – the church, church events, ministers, and other Christians. Because we are so busy, we have little time for a real prayer life and private study of God's Word. We are looking for someone else to provide the prayer and serve us the Word of God on a platter. Like the dog paddle, we soon tire of the constant movement. We burn ourselves out, and after reaching the point of exhaustion, we begin to sink again.

Spiritual Dead Man's Float

Another option is the dead man's float. The spiritual dead man's float requires us to lay still and do nothing. We do not do anything unless it is required of us. We might attend church on Sunday mornings, but there is no effort to offer our time, talents, or energy to God. We ritually pray in the evening and over our food and manage to sneak in a five-minute personal devotion time, but there is no real impact. As I said previously, the disadvantage of the dead man's float is that you have no control over the direction the winds and waves take you. Since there is no counteraction on our part, the spiritual dead man's float results in an unstable atmosphere. Where the winds and waves of your situation go is wherever your mind and heart will take you. The dead man's float puts you under the control of the wind and the waves. A wise woman once told me, "Your attitude determines your altitude." When you allow circumstances to dictate your attitude, you can never tell where your altitude will be on any given day. It does not take too many days of low altitude before you're drowning again.

Spiritual Freestyle

The only option with lasting results is swimming. Freestyle is the most effective and fastest swimming stroke. Swimming requires both action and effort on our part. We must first learn to swim properly to stay afloat and keep swimming to continue to stay afloat. One without the other is useless. Spiritual swimming includes simple steps familiar to us – praying, reading God's Word, and attending Bible study. Many of us have heard that these are the things we should do as growing Christians, but most of us will agree that they are the first things we stop doing when we are in a storm or beginning to drown. Simply stated: swimming involves getting in the presence of God. How we get into His presence and what we do in His presence may differ for each person, but we will never drown when we get into His presence. There is no drowning in the presence of God. Scripture says in Psalm 16:11, *"In thy presence is fullness of joy; at thy right hand, there are pleasures for evermore"* (KJV). With that being the case, the presence of God is the place we need to be when we are drowning.

Getting in His Presence

So how do we get into the presence of God? That sounds deeply religious, and when you are amid the raging storm and the waves seem like they are crashing over your head, the last thing you want to hear is religious talk. Personally, I find getting into His presence to be a difficult task because it requires a certain level of solitude. Solitude was the last thing I sought in the middle of the storm. I wanted noise and distraction - anything that would keep me from thinking about my circumstances. The reality is that it was satan who wanted me to feel this way. The devil knew that by keeping me in dog paddle mode, I would not get into God's presence, and, as a result, I would eventually drown. Jesus came so that we might have life and have it more abundantly (John 10:10 paraphrased); however, we must seek and know Jesus to receive that abundant life. I do not mean to know of Jesus or be acquainted with Him but to have an intimate relationship that allows Him to take us above our circumstances.

As I mentioned earlier, getting into the presence of God can differ for each person. For me, the most effective way is to find a quiet place with minimal distractions (if your house was anything like mine during my storm, that could be close to impossible). I begin with music - a gospel song with words that speak to my mood or encourage an atmosphere of praise to God. Sometimes it takes more than one song to get me into the place where God has my undivided attention. The song may be about how Jesus sacrificed His life on the cross for me, and that helps me get into a place where I am humbled and grateful. Other times, it may be a song that speaks to my discouragement, encourages me not to give up, and instructs me where to focus. At other times, it may be a song that offers praise and worship for who God is, how awesome He is, and how much He has done for me; then, I get into a place of praise. Whatever the song, I use music to set the mood.

The music leads to a period of praise and worship. Praise and worship can change your mood; it changes your attitude, takes your mind off your circumstances, and centers it on God. You must take your mind off the mountain and place it on the mountain mover.

However, it's not always as easy as this. While you might desire with all your heart to get in His presence, satan has other plans. He has no intention of making it easy for you to get in the presence of God because he is keenly aware of the power there. As you prepare to get in His presence, satan will distract you with everything from bills to laundry. Your mind will drift to the most mundane of issues to keep you from reaching that place. The key is to press on despite how you feel. As children, many of us were taught that what happens between God and us is a silent matter. But one weapon against the devil is to speak aloud. It is not that God cannot hear us in our silence, but when we speak aloud, we combat the devil's attack on our minds. Think of it this way: When you are in a conversation with someone, it is nearly impossible to speak intelligently and think about other things simultaneously. While speaking, your mind works to form what will come from your mouth.

Once you get into the place where you can sense the Spirit of God around you, the next phase has two steps: talk to God and listen. Both are equally important, but we often do all the talking and neglect to sit still and hear what He has to say. The concept of talking to God does not need much explanation, but I would simply emphasize the word "talk." Sometimes we get caught up in the idea of praying, and as a result, we use a lot of religious phrases – you know, church prayers. Instead, we need to talk to God about where we are, how we feel, and what's going on:

- "Okay, Lord, I feel like I'm drowning, and I need you to step in now."
- "Well, Father, I do not understand this storm. I feel like I've been under attack for a while now; where is my help?"
- "God, I'm trying to stay in your Word, pray, and worship you, but some days I am so discouraged that I do not want to get out of bed."

I can remember getting into the presence of God on many occasions and doing nothing but crying. The pain of my circumstances was so deep and real that I could not articulate to God how I felt. I could only tell Him that I hurt. I could only cry out and ask for Him to help me. There was no doubt that I was truly in His presence at these times. I felt the Spirit of God all around me, like a hand rubbing my back and shoulders, telling me everything would be all right.

We can say more through our tears than we can with a thousand words. Psalm 51:17 confirms that *"the sacrifices of God are a broken spirit; a broken and contrite heart, O God, thou wilt not despise"* (KJV). When pain and frustration reduce us to tears, we are usually at our most humble point, which is where God can get through to us. The apostle Paul says in 2 Corinthians 12:10, *"That is why for Christ's sake, I delight in weaknesses, in insults, in hardships, in persecutions, in difficulties. For when I am weak, then I am strong."* Just before this, Paul was addressing the issue of the thorn in his flesh that he wanted the Lord to remove. In 2 Corinthians 12:9, the Lord responds to Paul, *"My grace is sufficient for you, for my power is made perfect in weakness."*

Understand that God already knows we feel this way; He just wants to know if we trust Him enough to talk to Him. We must be careful not to spend twenty minutes complaining. You certainly wouldn't enjoy listening to anyone complain for twenty minutes, so why would God? He wants to know how we feel, but He also wants to know that we love Him despite how we feel. Now that we feel relief from laying all our cares and worries before the Master, we can sit quietly and listen to Him. Now, this is hard. The stress of work, the to-do list, the children, and the problems begin to flood the mind, but in our determination to hear from God, we must persist in our efforts. You may have to hum a tune, read a Psalm of praise to God, or just move into a moment of praise. Whatever you do, do not give up. Do not allow the devil to win by leaving your place of solitude until you believe you have gotten all you need from God at that time. In the book of Genesis, Jacob wrestled with an angel of the Lord and told him, *"I will not let you go unless you bless me"* (Genesis 32:26). Sometimes, we need to get in that secret place and tell God, "I will not let you go until you bless me."

Being in His presence gives us a rest that no amount of sleep can provide. It gives us peace that cannot be found in any yoga class. It gives us a sense of security that cannot be purchased with any amount of money. The presence of God is a place you must frequent if you are going to keep from drowning.

Speak Positive Things into Your Spirit

During a storm, negativity becomes an everyday occurrence. When there is a major event going on in one's life, it has a way of affecting everything else. The storm shifts a previously normal life into one of uncertainty, frustration, and pain: things that would normally be less significant become larger than life. At an otherwise normal time in life, a friend not returning a telephone call would not be an issue. Still, when you're amidst a storm, sensitivities are high, and that unreturned telephone call becomes a personal insult. The reality is that the friend probably has a very good reason for not returning the call, and the issue is not theirs but yours. You are transferring your feelings of insecurity from your circumstances to anything and everything in your path. Remember, this is not their problem. It's yours. You have allowed your insecurity to creep outside its boundaries. Your storm has you feeling weak and vulnerable; your weakness heightens your sensitivity to anything that might inflict pain. Rejection inflicts pain. So, you are over-sensitive to anything that feels like rejection, and you make small things larger than life.

We must speak positively to ourselves to launch a counterattack against the negativity that arises during a storm. It is literally speaking to oneself. All of us can be caught talking to ourselves when we are angry or upset, or it feels better to speak aloud. At first, it feels somewhat awkward and unnatural, but if you have ever been at the drowning stage, you are willing to try anything. As satan plants negative thoughts, negative people, and negative feelings inside of you, you must counteract that with the Word of God, Christian literature, prayer, and people who are encouragers. For example, it is common for us to use the phrase "I am depressed." If you continue telling yourself you are depressed, you will be depressed. You must turn that spirit around and tell yourself, "I am more than a conqueror." Remind yourself that the devil is a thief who comes to steal, kill, and destroy, but that Jesus came that you might have life and that more abundantly (John 10:10 paraphrased).

> *"The tongue has the power of life and death, and those who love it will eat its fruit."* – Proverbs 18:21

You must stand on Isaiah 54:17 – *"no weapon that is formed against thee shall prosper"* (KJV). Of course, there are deeper issues that surround clinical depression that require professional attention. I am only dealing with those who use the word "depressed" to describe the feelings they experience because of their temporary circumstances. For those who need more information on the issue of depression, I recommend seeking professional help. I also found valuable information in *Why Do I Feel So Down When My Faith Should Lift Me Up* by Grant Mullen, M.D.

The Word of God is the most positive thing you can speak into your spirit. Ephesians 6:17 refers to the Word of God as the sword of the Spirit, and Hebrews 4:12 describes it as *"living and active [and] sharper than any double-edged sword."* If you are in a battle, you most certainly want your sword to be sharp. The Word of God emphasizes, "sharper than any double-edged sword." If a sharp sword cuts, something sharper than a double-edged sword must be incredible. That is what you need for your battle. How do you use the Word of God as a weapon? Get it inside you - deep inside of you. Psalm 1:1-2 says, *"Blessed is the man who does not walk in the counsel of the wicked, or stand in the way of sinners, or sit in the seat of mockers. But his delight is in the law of the Lord, and on His law, he meditates day and night."* To get the Word of God inside us, we must meditate on it, study it, recite it, and memorize it. We must make our digestion of scripture as routine as the food we take into our bodies. Most of us rarely miss more than one meal a day unless we are fasting. Generally, we are ritualistic in our eating habits. Unless something stops us, our body clock will signal us to eat at approximately the same time each day. However, we may go days or months without spiritual food and then wonder why we are weak.

I am the first to admit that I had difficulty reading the Word consistently at times during my storm. Initially, I was working so hard to stay busy that I never had time (or should I say never made time). When I started to slow down and focus, I had difficulty figuring out what to read to encourage myself. I found that using an aid was the best solution. I found various Christian authors that met me where I was: Stormie Omartian, T.D. Jakes, Charles Swindoll, Thomas Tenney, and George McClung, to name a few. These authors provided a focus for me, challenged me, and gave me direction. If you want to keep your mind on Christ, you must fill yourself with that which will build your spiritual muscles, such as the instructions provided by the Psalmist:

- Psalm 119:11 – *"Thy word have I hid in mine heart that I might not sin against thee"* (KJV).
- Psalm 119:160 – *"Thy word is true from the beginning: and every one of thy judgments endureth forever"* (KJV).

Renew Your Mind

When recovering from a near-drowning experience, you must renew your mind with the help of God. Romans 12:2 states: *"**And do not be conformed to this world but be ye transformed by the renewing of your mind, that ye may prove what is, that good, and acceptable and perfect will of God**"* (KJV). Reversing the drowning process requires active participation on your part. During the drowning phase, you likely spent significant time dwelling on the negative and feeding neutral or negative things into your spirit. It is time to renew your mind. You must begin to fill your mind with things that positively affect your soul.

What does this mean? It means changing the type of things you watch on television. If it is your normal practice to watch talk shows with very little redeeming spiritual value, you need to turn off the television or turn to something more positive. If it is your normal course to listen to a popular radio station while driving in your car, you need to switch to Christian music. If you enjoy the latest popular novels or magazines, you need to find an inspirational Christian book that will meet you where you are. I am recommending a switch because you need to change your routine. Your old routine contributed to your drowning state. You need to adjust your thinking.

For example, the latest novel can often direct your mind to the material things in life that you do not have. The storyline may be about an inappropriate relationship that gives off an air of excitement or may simply suggest that it is okay to satisfy your needs and desires in whatever pleases you. These subtle messages can directly conflict with the Word of God and will contribute to your discontent with your circumstances. By renewing your mind with things pleasing to God, you actively work against the drowning process.

Philippians 4:8 says: *"**Finally brethren, whatsoever things are true, whatsoever things are honest, whatsoever things are just, whatsoever things are pure, whatsoever things are lovely, whatsoever things are of good report, if there be any virtue, and if there be any praise, think on these things"*** (KJV).

Fight Back

Drowning is easy and takes no effort. Floating requires minimal effort but gets you nowhere and eventually leads to drowning. Swimming requires that you take control of your situation and fight back. The devil can only win when we let him, and we let him by doing little or nothing. To fight back, you must know what weapons to use.

2 Corinthians 10:3-5 states: *"**For though we walk in the flesh, we do not war after the flesh; for the weapons of our warfare are not carnal, but mighty through God to the pulling down of strongholds. Casting down imaginations and every high thing that exalteth itself against the knowledge of God and bringing into captivity every thought to the obedience of Christ**"* (KJV). (Some versions paraphrase verse 3, "though we live in this world, we do not wage war as the world does.")

Our weapons include:

1. ***Praying*** – no matter how you feel, do not give up the practice of praying. Even if you simply tell the Lord that you do not know what to pray or ask Him to hear your thoughts - stay in touch with the Master. Do not unplug yourself from the Source.
2. ***Reading/studying the Word of God*** – I read somewhere that the Word of God has the answers to all of life's situations. You need to read the Word and take it further by memorizing it. Get it into your spirit, so it becomes a weapon against the

devil's attacks on your mind. You memorize your favorite song or information for your job, so why not the Word?
3. ***Making it a regular practice to get in His presence*** – Get quiet before God regularly. Do not allow the activities of the world to consume you to the point that you neglect time alone with God. Remember, **"in His presence, there is fullness of joy"** (Psalm 16:11). During a storm, joy is a precious commodity. Be selfish with your time. Make it clear to others that your time alone with God is not optional or negotiable - finding time alone with God is critical to your survival.
4. ***Speaking positive things into your spirit*** – commit to eliminating negative talk from your vocabulary. Each day, find something for which you can be grateful. Ask those closest to you to hold you accountable for what you say about yourself or your situation. Speak life into yourself. Tell yourself that you are "more than a conqueror,"[5] that "no weapon formed against you shall prosper,"[6] and "that all things work together for good to them that love God and are called according to His purpose."[7] Lay claim to God's Word, believing His promises are true.
5. ***Surrounding yourself with encouragers*** - During a storm, you need active encouragers. Passive friends simply will not do. When we are down, we are very good at throwing pity parties and crying out, "woe is me." None of this is helpful in any way; therefore, we need to be surrounded by Christians who refuse to join our pity party and encourage us to get up and stand tall through prayer and the Word of God. If you were drowning physically, you would not spend any energy listening to someone who was not trying to help you stay alive; therefore, react the same way in your spiritual life. Ask

---

[5] Romans 8:37
[6] Isaiah 54:17 (KJV)
[7] Romans 8:28

God to send you those who would encourage you spiritually to beat the devil at his own game.
6. ***Going out to eat*** – We love to go out to eat. Something about the atmosphere outside of our house makes food seem more enticing. The same can be true spiritually. While reading and studying your Word and spending quiet time with God, you must also go out to eat. Find a Bible study group or prayer group that you can feed off. Do not confine yourself to eating at home. Get spiritually fed by others in another setting. This extends to church attendance as well. I am not encouraging you to join another fellowship or to church hop, but when you are in a storm and everything seems so unsettled, attending church elsewhere or watching a different online service can be a blessing. Get out of your routine of sitting in the same seat or section, talking to the same people, and hearing the same choir. Let God take you out of your norm, put you in the unfamiliar, and watch Him speak to you in a new way. I dare you to be radical and take one Sunday to visit another fellowship. Make sure the fellowship you attend is a Bible-believing, Bible-teaching church. Ask people that you trust what church might be a good one to visit or watch online.

Chapter 5

Broken to Be Made Whole

Psalm 51:17 states: *"The sacrifices of God are a broken spirit; a broken and a contrite heart, O God, thou wilt not despise"* (KJV).

I am sure many have preached a similar message, but it was an anointed woman of God that preached this message during a women's retreat and changed my life. Sometimes a message is spoken, and it appears to have been specifically designed for you. This message was designed to open my eyes and see that my self-analysis differed from God's analysis. The concept is very simple. When we begin to soul-search, we look at ourselves and see behavior and feelings. When God begins His spring-cleaning process, He sees wounds and needs. I remember, as a young Christian, singing a song in church:

> Spirit of the living God
> Fall fresh on me
> Break me, melt me, fill me, use me.

I can truthfully say now that I had no idea what I was asking God to do, and if He had fulfilled my request, I would likely have lost my mind. I would never have been able to endure the breaking process at that stage in my life.

Breaking and Making Me

Being broken by God involves several steps.

- **Step 1:** God must first bring us to the point that we are so weak that we acknowledge our helplessness and hopelessness without Him.
- **Step 2:** He begins to identify the wounds in our lives that need healing. We are often wounded in areas we have not identified.
- **Step 3:** God begins cleaning out the wounds so they might heal properly.
- **Step 4:** He begins to create a whole person fit to fulfill His mission and vision.

The storm in my life served as the catalyst for God to begin the breaking process. I remember God allowing me to become so weak that, on the inside, I struggled with getting out of bed in the morning. In my mind, my storm should have ended six months earlier. Here I was, ten months into a storm that did not seem to have an end. Nothing about this storm made logical sense. The only clear and definite thing was that satan and his legion of demons had launched an attack that God, in his infinite wisdom, allowed.

I felt like a shaken bottle of soda about to explode. I remember being in a room full of people and feeling alone. I felt no one understood where I was, and no one could help me. I remember telling one of my closest friends that I felt like I was going to lose my mind. I could not understand why God had not stepped in and said "Peace" to the wind and the waves of my storm. He had done many miraculous things in the scriptures, but where was my miracle? My storm raged for almost a year, and God would not step in. All I wanted to know was WHY? But it was not my time yet. He had just begun His work.

Step one of the breaking process was complete. I attended the women's retreat for my church with a few words for my God – "If you do not meet me on this mountain, I am likely to lose my mind when I come down." I had truly reached the lowest emotional point of my life. However, as an independent and successful woman with a rewarding career, my emotional state was a well-kept secret. Like many, masking my pain and stress was a normal part of life. The Secret deodorant commercial says, "Never let them see you sweat." That was my mantra. I was too proud to ask for help and too independent to lean on anyone else. Some can share all that is going on with them; I am not one of those people. Sharing requires vulnerability, and vulnerability opens the window for hurt. My emotional walls were too thick to allow this to occur.

What God began on that retreat is almost unexplainable. Unbeknownst to me, God was moving me into step two of the breaking process. He used this weekend to reveal issues and wounds I did not know existed. He showed me behaviors and attitudes that were displeasing to Him and began to reveal the root cause of them. God began to open the wounds of the past that had healed incorrectly or had not healed at all.

My issues are likely to be different from those of others. We each struggle to overcome a unique set of situations and circumstances. Having been broken and made whole, I can share that my issues were control, pride, independence, and fear.

Control

God began with the issue of control. I felt I needed to have control over everything connected to me. Control meant I needed to influence anything in some way. Whenever possible, it was best that things went my way or were done as I needed. God stripped me of that control. He allowed me to be in a storm that I could do NOTHING to get out of and then allowed me to drop to such a low point emotionally that only He could bring me out. God began to take me through situations and circumstances that required me to consciously and verbally acknowledge that He is and will always be in control.

My professional career is a prime example of this principle in action. Upon completing my Master of Business Administration (MBA), I determined that with my newly earned degree and a license as a certified public accountant, I was marketable, and it was time to start my job search. I sent out ten to fifteen resumes for various positions, and some were identical to my current job. I immediately expected a flood of telephone calls for interviews. To my surprise, I did not receive one telephone call from an interested employer.

Initially, I decided it must be my resume format or the labor market. Then I began to feel inadequate and lose confidence in my abilities. After about nine months, God revealed that He had the stop sign up, and I did not see it. Despite all my education and marketability, God did not see fit to move me into a new job until 1½ years later. When God finally moved me to the new job, it was not the dream job I thought it would be; however, God knew it was the job I needed. The only thing I really enjoyed about the job was the salary and benefits, but God was clear that this was where He put me and where I would stay. God used that experience to show me that no degree, experience, or marketability can supersede His plan.

When God places us somewhere or in something, and we know it's God's will, it is in our best interest to simply relax in the knowledge that He is God and knows what He is doing. However, it is our nature to worry, complain, and try to fix things ourselves. I found myself complaining daily about my situation, although the job was financially keeping my household intact, and I knew that it was contrary to the scripture to complain. Part of my storm's circumstances included the loss of one income, and the income that remained came from the job God gave me, even though I disliked it. The apostle Paul in Philippians 4:11 says, *"I have learned to be content whatever the situation."* And Philippians 2:14 says, *"do everything without complaining or arguing."* I was so far away from this mindset that even reading those scriptures did not help. One day while driving to work, the Lord spoke to my heart and convinced me. I understood that this job, which I did not like, was a blessing from God financially. However, because it was not a place I liked or was comfortable with, I thanked God for the financial blessing and then talked about how much I did not like the job. The Spirit touched my heart one day and said:

> If someone gave you something you asked for, and you said thank you, but then you complained about it, how would the giver know you were grateful?

That gentle whisper from the Spirit of God told me that I was acting like a spoiled brat who received a gift from a parent and complained because it wasn't perfect. With that, I apologized to God and changed my tune. While I remained honest with God about how I felt about the job, I asked the Lord to help me see: 1) what He wanted me to learn while I was there, 2) what a financial blessing the job was to my family and others, and 3) what my assignment at this job was (did someone there need to see Christ through me?)

It is important that even in the most miserable situation, we look for the Savior. We can find Him and His purpose when we seek Him.

Pride

When the Lord identified pride as a problem, I must admit I was a bit surprised. I had never considered myself a prideful person, but God showed me that my façade was pride. My pride kept me from asking my friends for help or prayer. I would never share with anyone the feeling of helplessness and hopelessness that I felt because it would indicate vulnerability and weakness. Pride tells you that you can accomplish anything yourself and that you do not need any help. Proverbs 16:18 states, *"pride goes before destruction, a haughty spirit before a fall."*

Pride is not always easy to identify. Often, we associate pride with the verbal expression of self-achievement or people who focus on themselves. Maybe, like me, you do not see pride as a particular issue for you. Answer this question honestly: can you share your experiences, storms, or disappointments with others who may benefit from your victory? If the answer is no and the reason is that you do not want anyone to know your struggles or you do not want anyone to think anything negative about you, you *may* have pride issues.

Independence

Closely linked with pride was the issue of independence. Pride would not allow me to admit I needed someone. As a thinking person, I rationalized my pride by telling myself that Psalm 118:8 says, *"it is better to trust in the Lord than to put confidence in man"* (KJV), but the reality was I did not want anyone to see how broken I was. I was unwilling to be vulnerable to any human being by exposing all my hurt and pain. I was too independent to rely on anyone or, more accurately, to allow God to use anyone to intervene on His behalf. The world sees independence as a good thing: being able to stand on your own two feet. But God never asked us to stand on our own feet, only to stand girded with the armor of God (Ephesians 6). In fact, to the contrary, in Proverbs 3:5-6, Solomon tells us to *"Trust in the Lord with all thine heart and lean not unto thine own understanding. In all thy ways acknowledge him, and he shall direct thy path."* (KJV). Translation: do not do anything without checking with God.

If being dependent on God were solely the issue, that would be one thing, but the pride issue discussed above acted as a driving force for being independent of everyone. The concept of dependence on others requires a level of vulnerability and is not the same as dependence on God. Dependence on God means total blind faith and trust in Him - not making a single move without Him. Dependence on others is about creating intimate relationships, and intimacy in a relationship is critical to the growth and depth of that relationship. By intimacy, I am not referring to physical contact but the emotional bond that develops when two people share thoughts, feelings, and experiences. While uncovering pride that caused independence, God opened the wound that prohibited the development of intimate relationships. I could boast of a few close relationships, but most lacked the level of vulnerability that makes for great relationships. God's identification process revealed that my independence from others had deeper roots. More than pride and not allowing anyone to see my brokenness, my pride was driven by fear.

Fear of Rejection

To protect my independent status, I created emotional walls. The emotional walls prohibited my relationships from having the intimacy that the love of 1 Corinthians 13 describes. There must be a vulnerability to have intimacy in any relationship. God showed me that my refusal to be vulnerable directly resulted from fear. My fear was two-fold: I was afraid of allowing someone to be close enough to have enough information and ammunition to hurt me, and I also had a fear of rejection. In intimate relationships, parties share information and feelings that are very personal and private. Such sharing is risky if one of the persons receiving such information does not handle it properly.

Too often, human nature gets the best of us, and we think it harmless to share just one story or piece of information that was told to us in confidence. Have you ever had someone tell you something and say, "Do not tell anyone because she or he told me not to tell anyone?" My immediate reaction is to ask, "Then why are you telling me?" We seem to think that telling just one person does not break the other party's confidence. Let me give a word of advice to those who may think this way: You Are Breaking Someone's Trust In You As Soon As You Tell Anyone But God!

For a private person, fear of information leaks can impact interactions with others. I have experienced situations where the information I have shared returns to me, often in a distorted version, when I know, I only shared it with one or two persons. A natural reaction to such an experience might be not to share any information with those persons. But, driven by my fear and tendency toward extremism in protecting my heart, I chose to refrain from sharing information, period. I do not suggest that sharing personal thoughts, feelings, or experiences with many people is the ideal alternative. However, some relationships could be a blessing from God and are never truly developed because of this fear. Fear can hinder relationships and prohibit intimacy in new relationships.

I learned that it was difficult for me to pursue relationships that might be good for me spiritually because of two fears: 1) the person would behave in a manner that indicated disinterest in such a relationship, or 2) the person would pretend to be interested out of obligation or the need to "be nice." In both cases, the result was a feeling of rejection. Whether the other parties' intention was rejection was not particularly relevant because my interpretation drove the fear. Fear is most often rooted in circumstances of the past. They may be childhood experiences that have followed you into adulthood or recent experiences with fresh wounds. Fear is real and can control one's actions and reactions.

If fear is an area that you struggle with, it is important to identify what you fear and then try to find the source of the fear. For many of us, soul searching will reveal all that we need to know about our fears. For others, a trusted friend or professional counselor could be a better route. Whichever route you choose, I recommend identifying and facing your fears to become whole.

The Pain of Cleaning

The identification process continued after my return from the retreat, and then the painful part began. God began to clean out the wounds. The process can be likened to breaking a bone in your body, having it heal incorrectly, then having the doctor re-break it so it can heal properly. It is that re-breaking process that hurts the most. As another example, imagine a deep cut that becomes infected. The doctor may have to remove the infection with a scalpel, then use an antiseptic to clean the wound. The pain from the cleaning solution may sting for a bit, even after the wound is cleaned out. My cleaning process involved pain, tears, and much talking to God.

Coming Out of Your Comfort Zone

The commonality in all the soul-searching and spring cleaning was that God drew me out of my comfort zone. Everyone has a place and space in their lives where they are comfortable. In that place, they have a circle of people where we are comfortable. We share information with some in our circle, others, we share feelings. In either case, the comfort zone puts everything into a neat compartment. For many of us, coming out of our comfort zone is an undesirable option. We have conditioned ourselves to be so closed and protected that we are unwilling to risk coming out of our comfort zone. Unfortunately, our comfort zone is usually a hindrance to carrying out God's will. Becoming whole means venturing outside that area that has been safe for so long and moving into the place where God is calling you.

You begin to change in the middle of a real storm. In a storm, we look for comfort, but that comfort may very well be outside of our comfort zone. Coming out of your comfort zone is a scary and risky process. However, you will quickly discover that the area outside your comfort zone has much to offer. God will use a storm to bring us out of our comfort zone so that we can grow because our comfort zone restricts our growth to within its confines. The sky is the limit when God takes us outside that zone.

When I reached an extremely low point emotionally in my storm, God took that opportunity to introduce some things to me that were outside my comfort zone. My comfort zone had always been marked by relationships with little intimacy and controlled emotions. Even in some of my closest friendships, I had the "never let them see you sweat" mentality. I believed that the more people knew about you, the more deeply they could hurt you. That way of thinking, while considered safe, is extremely limiting. Some truly wonderful relationships may be missed if your comfort zone is like mine was, where limited intimacy and controlled emotions were the order of the day.

The concept of Halloween is characterized by dressing up in costumes with masks so that one cannot be recognized. The everyday world operates with the same philosophy of wearing masks so that we are not recognized. Many of us wear one mask at work, a different one at church, and a different one in our social circles. These masks hide the feelings or characteristics we do not want others to see. While masks serve a purpose in life, God is not interested in our masks. When our need to wear masks gets in the way of His divine will, He will remove them. That's what happened in the storm: God forced my hand and began to peel away the layers of masks like an onion because my masks were hindering how He might use me. When He removed the masks, I could see Him more clearly, and, more importantly, I could hear Him more clearly.

Chapter 6

Hearing God in the Storm

One of the biggest problems in the storm is knowing what to do next. When you examine the Old Testament stories, God always knew how to get the attention of His servants. God got Jonah's attention when he was in the belly of the fish. God got Gideon's attention when he decreased his troops from thousands to three hundred. God got Jehoshaphat's attention when the report came that a vast army was approaching.

One of the reasons it is so hard to hear God in the storm is that there is so much surrounding noise. In general, we live in a society that encourages noise. Fast and noisy is the way we live. When the storm surrounds us, the noise becomes louder. We try to drown out the effects of the storm with more noise. Scripture says, *"**Be still and know that I am God**."*[8] Yet, during the storm, we move faster, create more noise, and, as a result, we cannot hear God.

In our attempt to stay out of depression, we keep ourselves busy doing things. However, these "things" do not change the circumstances; they only distract our attention temporarily. It can

---
[8] Psalm 46:10

be likened to someone who uses alcohol or drugs to escape life's problems. After the high wears off, the problems still exist. This method of dealing with the problem is not a solution but more like an ineffective alternative to dealing with the problem head-on; so, it is with noise and busyness. Often the storm is designed or allowed by God to get our attention. Unfortunately, we move in the opposite direction. We spend less time with God or certainly no additional time with God. We find numerous other things to keep us busy and distracted. We neglect the areas of our lives that need to be cultivated during a storm.

When we should be on our knees praying, we are watching television. When we should be reading the Word of God, we are surfing the Internet or engaging in the black hole of social media. I am guilty of this myself. Because so much of my life was filled with tension, anxiety, and general unhappiness while the storm was brewing, I latched on to anything that I enjoyed that relaxed me or took my mind off my situation. I began spending too much time surfing the Internet, always looking for something.

There was nothing overtly negative about surfing the Internet. Sometimes, I think my subconscious was looking for the answer to my storm on the web. I spent time looking for a new job, a new house, things to buy, and something to occupy my mind. I enjoyed those online auctions where you are bidding against unknown people. It thoroughly distracted me and brought out my competitive spirit. Of course, winning meant it would cost me money, but since I did not win very often, that never became a problem. The time I wasted on the Internet was time I could have devoted to the One who had the answers - the Lord. I could have been writing this book instead of playing games on the computer.

Difficulty Hearing?

I believe that God had my attention in the storm. I had deepened my relationship with Him. However, He did not have my undivided attention. I was using some of God's time to fulfill my desire to escape by almost any means necessary. I say almost because I had reached a level spiritually where blatant sin was not an option. I was unwilling to indulge in a sinful lifestyle to distract my mind from my storm. I was, and still am, very afraid of God.

So, what was missing for me? I was having difficulty hearing God because I was not always listening. Sometimes when someone is talking, you can hear them, but you are not really listening. While your ears can hear sound resonating from someone's lips, your mind has taken you into another dimension, and you do not listen to what that person is saying. That is how I was with God. I would hear Him say something to me, and I would not respond because I was too distracted or it didn't make complete sense to me, so I figured it must not be God. I began to wonder if it was God speaking to me or whether it was my thoughts or desires talking to me. But God is not the author of confusion (1 Corinthians 14:33). When God has something to say, He gives you the direction He wants you to go. He is very clear in His message.

Earlier, I talked about my job search after receiving my MBA. The part I left out was that during that year and a half of searching for a job, the Lord spoke to me and told me that He wanted me to go out on my own. He was calling me to start a consulting practice in finance and accounting. Initially, I was not sure that it was God speaking, but he kept sending me confirmations until August 20, 1999, when I wrote in my journal that God had confirmed I should become my own boss. I had started consulting on the side in addition to my full-time job and loved it, but God was calling me to do more. I reduced my schedule at my full-time job from five to three days per week and began consulting on the other two days. Things were going along well, and I was adjusting to being an entrepreneur.

Suddenly, in January of 2000, the storm hit and my life changed. I suspended my consulting, thinking that I would resume when the storm was over; it was not supposed to last long. When it appeared that the storm was taking on a life of its own, I (and the key word here is "I") determined that consulting was too big of a risk with its unpredictable income and loss of company benefits. I needed to make sure my family had at least one stable income. So, I resumed my search for a full-time job that would provide the professional and intellectual challenge that I was looking for, combined with the financial security of a biweekly paycheck, which does not come with independent consulting.

Just Not Listening?

Psalm 37:4 says, *"Delight yourself in the Lord, and He will give you the desires of your heart."* Even though I had received confirmation that God wanted me to be out on my own professionally, I did not have the faith to step out just yet. God knew that I was not quite ready, so He laid out an offer I could not refuse. The job He offered in September 2000 was with a major insurance company, and the offer contained everything I had always dreamed of in my professional career: an esteemed title, a six-figure salary, a signing bonus, an annual bonus, stock options, and the potential for advancement. On the company's organizational chart, there were only two people between my position and the company's CEO. It seemed surreal to a Black woman raised in the inner city of Boston. However, God is no respecter of persons. I was trying to serve him faithfully, and he saw fit to give me the desires of my heart. Because His timing is always perfect, the offer came on the day the storm turned for the worse, reducing us to one salary. I knew the offer was from God;

He would take care of us financially through the storm, and He did just that.

That is just the beginning of the story. One of our problems as finite human beings is that we do not realize that what we want is not always what is best for us. God always wants what is best for us, and that was the case for me. After accepting this outstanding offer, it was not long before I realized that this was not the place for me. By the end of the second month, I was completely miserable. I was making great money, but I would have rather been a street sweeper than go to my office each morning. So, with the storm around me appearing very dark, I was now entering a storm within a storm. While the big storm may have been a "you're not quite there" storm, this new storm was a "disobedient" storm. I was now in the belly of a very large fish, and my fish was a multibillion-dollar insurance company.

The Jonah in Us

Look at Jonah. God was clear in His instruction to Jonah to go to Nineveh and preach a message of salvation. Jonah heard God, but He was not listening. God was not saying what Jonah wanted to hear, so Jonah went in the opposite direction to Joppa. Now it's funny when we read the story of Jonah, and we think to ourselves, "What audacity did Jonah have to be so defiant and outwardly disobedient to God?" A little self-analysis would quickly help us to see that Jonah is not God's only willfully disobedient child.

We have all heard God on an issue where we did nothing or did our own thing. The issue may not have been as large as Jonah's. God may have simply told us to reach out to some brother or sister or go to someone who offended us and try to reconcile. Due to our stubbornness and pride, we easily pretended that we did not hear God, or better yet, we heard Him and then went to others to get their opinions on what God said. This is classic for many women; we consistently get opinions from our girlfriends on everything. However, what can any of our friends add after God has spoken on an issue?

Maybe God is calling you to some area or ministry that is uncomfortable. We can be much like Moses in Exodus 3:7-11 when God instructed him to go to Pharaoh to speak concerning the Israelites. Moses made every excuse he could think of to convince God that he was not the guy. I sounded much like Moses when I heard God's call to write this book. I have a few friends who have heard God's call on their lives to preach but do not like the call. While you cannot see them running to Joppa like Jonah, they pretend to be hard of hearing.

The Growth from the Belly

Sometimes our message is not as clear as Jonah's, but in hindsight, we can see that God was instructing us in a certain manner, and we were not quite getting the picture. An analogy about the belly of the fish creates clarity. Just as a large fish was waiting for Jonah when he was thrown off the boat, God has positioned large fish in our lives. The belly of the fish is not a pleasant place to be, but it does serve a purpose. If you can just imagine all the junk the fish swallowed in the previous 24 hours, not to mention the smell inside the fish, Jonah must have thought that death would be better. It was in the belly of the fish that Jonah recognized the sovereignty of God. He realized that disobeying did not mean that God would go away. It was in the belly that Jonah learned humility. Seriously, how defiant can you be sitting in the belly of a fish with last night's dinner floating around you? It was in the belly that Jonah got real with God. Jonah had nothing else to do in the belly but pray, so He talked to God about what was really in his heart.

It took being trapped in the belly of the fish for Jonah to reach that critical point of no return in his relationship with God. After three days in the belly, Jonah was willing to obey God's call, even though he did not like it or agree with it. That is important to remember: God is not looking for our agreement or approval of the assignments He places on us. We often do not agree with or like what God calls us to. My advice is: Get Over It! God expects us to carry out His mission, and it will not always meet our fancy.

Jonah did not want to go to Nineveh to preach the message of salvation because he knew that a revival would overtake the city. Now, isn't that bold of Jonah to believe he could predict where a revival would break out? Do not look down too hard on Jonah; we do this daily. We have an opinion about everything and sometimes everybody. For example, when people are not a part of our group or clique, we are not quick to invite them to join our project or ministry. We, like Jonah, believe that we are entitled to our opinions and decisions – even with God.

That is why God created the belly. God designed the belly for us because He knows we will need a little help getting to the point when we are ready to accept His call. The belly provides us with time -- the time it takes to reach that point when we truly hear God. We reach our lowest point inside the belly. After three days and three nights in the belly of the fish, *"**Jonah prayed unto the Lord his God out of the fish's belly. And said, 'I cried by reason of mine affliction unto the Lord, and he heard me; out of the belly of hell cried I, and thou heardst my voice*"* (Jonah 2:1-2 KJV). The belly is designed to be an experience that will bring you to the point of saying, "All to Jesus, I surrender."

In the story of Joseph, his experience was also unpleasant, like Jonah's belly experience. It developed not out of disobedience but was God's predestined and strategic plan for Joseph. It was designed to get Joseph to surrender his entire being and walk in His calling. However, Joseph must have felt like he was in the belly of a fish when his experience took place in Potiphar's jail. [9] Joseph was in a position where he had God's favor. He was not blatantly disobedient, but he was not ready for God's assignment. God was completely and absolutely in total control of Joseph's situation. That is the reality of a belly situation; we cannot do anything to get ourselves out of it, whether or not we did anything to get ourselves into it.

There is one important element of Joseph's experience: Joseph had God's favor because he trusted and honored God despite his circumstances. When Joseph's brothers sold him into slavery to the Egyptians, he found favor with God and prospered living in Potiphar's house (Genesis 39:2). Then Joseph was accused of trying to sleep with Potiphar's wife and was sent to jail. Still, while Joseph was in prison, God granted him favor in the eyes of the prison warden (Genesis 39:21). After Joseph interpreted Pharoah's dream, he was placed in charge of the Pharaoh's palace (Gen. 41:40). Joseph maintained his integrity and devotion to God, so God continued to bestow his favor upon Joseph.

Hearing and seeing God in the storm was an important part of Joseph's unwavering trust in God. Because Joseph had a personal relationship with God, he knew that any situation he found himself in was in the hands of God; therefore, he never needed to take matters into his own hands. When we fail to hear the voice of God in a storm, we make the mistake of taking matters into our own hands and solving the problem our way. When we recognize that the battle belongs to God, we do not need to try to fight the battle using our strength.

The reason that the belly is an opportunity for growth is that it forces you to focus. The belly makes a statement that says, "You are here because God is trying to tell you something. Now sit up and listen, and maybe you'll get out." How we use the time in the

---

[9] Genesis chapters 37 - 42

belly is up to us. We can sit around and have a pity party, hoping God will release us from the belly out of sheer pity, or we can use that time in the belly to develop an intimate relationship with God. Since the belly will likely bring you to the lowest point of your life, that is the perfect place to meet your God. I am not saying that you cannot meet God in any other place or even that you have not met God previously, but when you are in the belly of the fish and you begin to feel like the walls are closing in on you, you can meet Him in a way you never have before.

The belly is designed to make you desperate for God. When Jonah was in the belly of the fish, he became desperate for God: *"In my distress, I called to the Lord, and he answered me"* (Jonah 2:2). That is exactly what God wanted - a desperate servant. When we are desperate, God can do something with us. The Old and New Testaments are full of examples of saints who were desperate for God and cried out to Him, and He heard them. 1 Samuel 1 tells the story of Hannah, barren and desperately wanting a child. Year after year, she cried because God had closed her womb. She went to the house of God and prayed that if God gave her a son, she would dedicate the child to him for all the days of her life. While praying, the priest, Eli, saw her lips moving but heard no words and accused her of being drunk. Hannah responded to the man of God, *"I am a woman who is deeply troubled. I have not been drinking wine or beer; I was pouring out my soul to the Lord. Do not take your servant for a wicked woman; I have been praying here out of my great anguish and grief"* (1 Samuel 1:15-16).

When you are desperate, you do not care what people think or say. You are willing to put dignity in the closet if it means getting the attention of God. Hannah wanted God's favor, and she wanted God's attention. Eli did not have a clue; he thought Hannah was drunk. I heard my Godmother preach one day: she was not drunk; she was desperate. In Hannah's desperate state, God heard her and granted her favor.

The woman with the issue of blood in the gospel of Mark reveals a similar desperate state of mind. In Mark chapter 5, beginning at verse twenty-five, we read of a woman who was subjected to bleeding for twelve years. The Bible is not explicit on exactly why or how she was bleeding, but just imagine bleeding from any part of your body for twelve years. The story indicates that she had seen many doctors, and her problem only worsened. Any exegetical preacher would tell you that, based on the culture of her day, she was considered ceremonially unclean. She would have been ostracized for twelve years of being considered less than a clean woman. She experienced twelve years of people staring, murmuring, laughing, and pointing at her — twelve years that likely caused as much emotional pain and scarring as physical.

There is no question that when this woman heard that Jesus was in town healing the sick and raising the dead, she was desperate to see him. She pressed her way through the crowd and touched Jesus' cloak. *"She thought, 'If I just touch his clothes, I will be healed"* (Mark 5:28). She was so desperate for help from Jesus that she believed there was enough power in even his clothes to heal her. After she touched him, Jesus immediately felt that power had gone out of him and responded, *"Who touched my clothes?"* (Mark 5:30). Whether Jesus knew who touched him before He asked the question is an issue for the theologians to debate. My guess is it was a rhetorical question. However, Jesus wanted to point out to the disciples and the crowd that this woman, in desperation, believed in His healing power so deeply that she felt she only needed to touch His clothes to be healed. She did not even need His full attention and did not need any holy oil, the pastor, the elders, or the deacons. She only needed to get close enough to touch His garment. She was desperate for the Master, and her desperation got Jesus' attention. In verse 34 of this chapter, Jesus says, **"Daughter, your faith has healed you. Go in peace and be freed from your suffering."** It is our desperation that gets the attention of God, and, unfortunately, we often do not get to that point of desperation until we have been in the belly for some time.

Another example of desperation in the gospels is in Luke 5:18-20, where Jesus teaches the Pharisees and law teachers. A group of men got desperate for their friend. *"Some men came carrying a paralytic on a mat and tried to take him into the house to lay him before Jesus. When they could not find a way to do this because of the crowd, they went up on the roof and lowered him on his mat through the tiles into the middle of the crowd, right in front of Jesus"* (Luke 5:18-19). Now, these men were not concerned about the agenda of the day. Jesus was not in the process of healing; he was teaching the religious elite. The fact that the room was crowded would have caused many of us to turn away and seek Jesus another day, but these men were desperate. Desperate times call for desperate measures. Climbing onto the roof carrying a person with paralysis on a mat is risky. What would have happened if they had dropped him? What would have happened if one of the men slipped and fell from the roof? What would have happened if they fell through the roof onto the people? Whatever the risk, these men were desperate enough to go for it. It was their desperation for Jesus that got His attention.

Jeremiah 29:12 says that we will find Him when we seek God with our whole heart. These men sought Jesus with all that they had. The woman with the issue of blood, as the Bible refers to her, risked everything to touch Jesus' clothes. Hannah poured her heart out to God and was accused of being drunk to get what she wanted from God. Sometimes you must risk violating what is "politically correct" to get what you need from God. God honors us in our contrite brokenness (Psalm 51:17).

My Belly Experience

After three months at my new job, I thought of resigning. Unfortunately, that was not a real option because, as I said, it was the only income for the household. In addition, there were financial ramifications to leaving before my first anniversary; therefore, with money as the focal point, I was stuck in the belly of the fish for a minimum of nine more months. In pregnancy, nine months does not seem very long, but when you work at a job that makes you completely and thoroughly unhappy, nine months seems more like nine years.

But how could this job be the belly of a fish when God had placed me here? That was very simple. He gave me what I asked for in a new job, but what I was asking for was not what He was calling me to do. He called me to start my own business, but because I lacked the faith to take the step, He gave me the dream I desired. I was about to learn a very important lesson: make sure your dreams line up with God's will.

I remember sitting in my office many days, crying to God to deliver me from my miserable situation. I remember my frustration with God for allowing me to suffer in the belly when there was a hurricane swirling in my life. But it was during that time in the belly, in that small office with no windows, that I spent every morning in prayer and study of the Word to fortify myself for the day. It was in the belly that I began to write the first pages of this book. It was in the belly that I began to understand what it was to be in a spirit of prayer all day long. I moved from the traditional framework of prayer in the morning or evening to praying throughout the day as the situation called for it. I created a deeper and more intimate relationship with God out of my desperate need for His deliverance. I began my belly experience feeling depressed and defeated, but by the time I reached eight months on the job, I learned how to use the weapons of my warfare. I learned how to combat the devil's attacks using my spiritual weapons.

Knowing the weapons of war was the missing piece. I was feeding my spirit with the scriptures and other Christian reading material and fighting the devil's attacks on my mind by speaking positively to myself. There were many days when I woke up in the morning depressed that it was another workday, but I learned to get out of bed by thanking God for another day and the opportunity to serve Him and asking Him for the strength to make it to the end of the day. I would be untruthful if I said that I was always up or that it was easy once I learned to use my weapons. Even after I learned how to fight satan, I still had days when I needed my lifeguard to pull me up because I was beginning to drown. In those instances, it was more of a temporary slip and not the drowning experience that occurred at the beginning of my storm.

If you find yourself in the belly of the fish because you have failed to be obedient to the call of Christ, first recognize that you will not be released from the belly immediately. Just because you acknowledge your disobedience to God and vow to remedy the situation does not mean that you will be released from the belly at that time. If there are lessons that God wants you to learn, He may use the belly, where He has your attention, to reinforce His point.

The second thing to recognize about being in the belly is that whining and complaining about the conditions of the belly will not help your situation or release you. The belly will not be enjoyable, so get used to it. It is in your best interest to figure out why you are in the belly and what you need to learn before you can get out and focus on that. Any other energy you exert is likely to be a waste.

The final thing to know about the belly is that no matter how long it lasts, if you come out the right way, it will be one of the most painful yet spiritually advancing experiences of your life. *"**And the Lord commanded the fish, and it vomited Jonah onto the dry land**"* (Jonah 2:10). If you seek God with all your heart, you will find that after you are out of the belly, your relationship with the Father will never go back to business as usual. You will only desire to go even deeper and become more intimate with God.

Jeremiah 29:12-13 says, *"**Then you will call upon me and come and pray to me, and I will listen to you. You will seek me and find me when you seek me with all your hear**t."*

Sometimes, when God gets your attention in the belly and has you fully focused on Him, He will instruct you to do something that makes absolutely no sense. You begin to wonder if you have a hearing issue. Some of God's most awesome work comes from seemingly strange directives.

Chapter 7

Crazy Trust

"Thou wilt keep him in perfect peace whose mind is stayed on thee because he trusteth in thee" (Isaiah 26:3 KJV).

"And without faith, it is impossible to please God, because anyone who comes to Him must believe that He exists and that He rewards those who earnestly seek Him" (Hebrews 11:6)

Noah - Crazy or Crazy Trust?

Crazy trust is when God calls you to do something that makes no sense to the average logical mind. For example, in Genesis 6, God called Noah to build an ark large enough to accommodate his family, plus two animals of every kind. We all know that the purpose of this ark was to save them from the flood, and it sounds logical to build an ark that would float on top of the water. However, three very small points make it illogical. Firstly, there is no indication in scripture that Noah was a carpenter. All my research has revealed that Noah's trade was agriculture; therefore, it was not within his natural talent to build a 40-cubit foot ark from the ground up. Secondly, since God is all-powerful, why did Noah have to build the ark? If God wanted to keep Noah and his family and two animals of every kind alive, why couldn't he simply build a safe haven where the water would not touch them? It did not make sense for Noah to spend years building an ark that God could have created in seconds. Finally, and most significantly, it was not raining. Many theologians agree that it had never rained on earth yet. So, why would Noah need to build an ark if there were no signs of rain?

From the human perspective, these three points are illogical, and most of us would request some explanation before we act. But let's step outside the human perspective and look at these issues through our spiritual eyes. Firstly, Noah was not a carpenter by trade, so constructing this ark could be considered a miracle. The size of this ark is said to be about the length of a football field. Occasionally, I will tinker around the house, putting things together or repairing something, but there is no way I could build a house because I am not trained to do this. Because Noah was not a carpenter, it would be clear to him and everyone around him that he could not build that ark alone.

The glory belonged to God for building the ark and saving Noah's family and the animals, and by having an amateur build the ark, everyone would know who the ultimate builder was. If you have some tasks that God has placed in front of you that are totally outside of your ability, be assured that He will complete the work through you, but He wants you and everyone else to understand where the glory belongs. If you thought you completed the task on your own, you might take credit instead of attributing the glory to God.

The second point is why didn't God just make the ark appear or build a safe haven for Noah's family and the animals? If God had simply given Noah and his family a place to go, the level of faith required by Noah would not have been significant. For Noah to walk onto an already-built ark because of a potential flood was low risk. If the flood had never happened, Noah could simply walk off the ark with the attitude of "better safe than sorry." However, for Noah to spend years building an ark for a flood, which from a human perspective was not guaranteed to occur, took crazy faith. Noah had to truly believe God at His word to begin this massive task without concrete proof that he was not wasting his time. That is the definition of faith. Hebrews 11:1 states, *"Now faith is the substance of things hoped for, the evidence of things not seen"* (KJV).

If God had put the ark on the earth for Noah to see, Noah would have had some evidence that God intended to bring the flood. When God is looking for crazy trust, He's not interested in giving you concrete evidence to lean on. When He calls you to take a step out on faith, He doesn't usually let you see the step. If it's going to be crazy trust, you must be willing to step out into nothing. You must believe in Hebrews 11:6 that God will reward those who diligently seek Him. This type of trust is crazy because it doesn't make sense to the logical mind. You must look through your spiritual eyes if you are going to see even a glimpse of what God sees.

Our final point is that there was no rain, so why did Noah build the ark? The answer is simple: God told him to. The Lord told Noah that the earth would be destroyed by flood. Noah had two choices: ignore God since His command did not make sense, or exhibit crazy trust by building an ark in dry weather. By building the ark, Noah risked ridicule from others because he was the only one who had heard from God that the earth would be destroyed by flood. In addition, Noah also risked that maybe it would not rain, and he would spend years building the ark for nothing. Imagine the scene if it did not rain: 1) Noah would be ridiculed for the rest of his life for building the ark and leaving it sitting in his backyard, 2) his family would begin to question his sanity, considering he claimed to have heard from God, 3) people would begin to question the validity of the God Noah served, and 4)

Noah's mental state would likely be severely affected by the aftermath.

But we all know the ending to the story: Noah trusted in God and built the ark before the flood came. Noah had crazy trust. Noah knew what many of us need to figure out: "***God is not a man that He should lie***" (Numbers 23:19.) If He said it's going to rain, then we need to be like Noah and just build the ark. Too often, God instructs us to do something, and we have doubts, questions, and issues that hold up His program. We will even pull a Jonah move and run in the opposite direction. We may have difficulty in our faith; we cannot just believe that God will do what He said He would do. Imagine the result if Noah did not build the ark. There would be no you or me, but God chose Noah because he was righteous and found favor before him – God knew Noah would be obedient.

Abraham – Crazy or Crazy Trust?

Continuing our discussion of crazy trust, we look at Abraham (Genesis 22). God commanded Abraham to take Isaac, his only son born of Sarah, to the top of the mountain and sacrifice him. This was an illogical request on God's part because Isaac was the heir that God had promised to Abraham, and God gave Isaac to Abraham and Sarah in their old age. After promising this son to Abraham, with whom God would establish His covenant, God tells Abraham to take Isaac up the mountain to sacrifice him.

Some of us have read this story repeatedly and agree that "yes" would not have been our first answer. No matter how badly our children get on our nerves, we would not be willing to obey a command from God to sacrifice them. I am a businessperson by trade and not a theologian, but I imagine that Abraham probably did not tell Sarah where he was taking Isaac. Any mother reading this story would agree that if our husband came to us declaring that God told him to kill our firstborn, we would probably ask him how crazy he was and then snatch our son back. Abraham trusted God. He trusted God in such a powerful and crazy way that he took his son to be sacrificed with the attitude that the sovereign God of the universe knew what He was doing and would handle the situation.

In verse 5 of chapter 22, Abraham says to his servants, "*Stay here with the donkey while the boy and I go over there. We will worship and then we will come back to you.*" Why did Abraham say that when the Lord had already indicated that Isaac was to be sacrificed? The reason is clear: Abraham took God at His word. In Genesis chapter 17, verse 19, God declares to Abraham, "*Yes, but your wife Sarah will bear you a son, and you will call him Isaac. I will establish my covenant with him as an everlasting covenant for his descendants after him.*" If God were to establish a long-lasting covenant with Isaac, then sacrificing him at a young age would be contrary to this promise.

Abraham knew that God's promises were true and that the sacrifice on that day would not be his son Isaac. In verse 8 of chapter 22, Isaac asked his father where the lamb was for the burnt offering, and Abraham responded, *"God himself will provide the lamb for the burnt offering, my son."* Abraham did not know the solution to the missing piece of the puzzle, but He knew that God already had the answer. Crazy trust means not knowing the answer but believing God knows the answer and acting in a manner that indicates that you trust Him.

Gideon – Crazy or Crazy Trust?

In Judges 7, we find Gideon and the Israelites up against the Midianites. The Lord spoke to Gideon in verse 2, *"**You have too many men for me to deliver Midian into their hands. In order that Israel may not boast against me that her own strength has saved her…**"*. I am not sure about you, but if I'm going to enter a war, having too many men does not seem to pose a problem. My philosophy is that the more, the merrier when it comes to a battle.

As the story continues, God reduces Gideon's troops from 22,000 to 10,000, then down to 300. However, God tells us up front why He is going to reduce the troops: *"**In order that Israel may not boast against me that her own strength has saved her**"* (Judges 7:2). God knows our hearts. He knows that if we believe we have everything it takes to accomplish something for Him when we accomplish it, the glory will go to the wrong place.

When God reduced the troops from 22,000 to 300, He knew that there was no way that Israel could boast of what it had done. But to put the icing on the cake, the Midianites' defeat came from blowing trumpets and smashing jars. The Israelites did not lift a finger against the Midianites. They did as God commanded and simply blew 300 trumpets. Upon the sound of 300 trumpets, God caused the Midianites to turn on each other with their own swords. Now how exactly does one win a battle by blowing trumpets? That makes no sense. But when God is in charge, anything is possible.

Gideon was not crazy; he trusted God at His word. The Lord told Gideon that He would deliver the Midianites into the hands of Israel. Standing on that word, Gideon trusted God by going out with only 300 men, trumpets, and jars. Without crazy trust, you cannot win a battle with trumpets. If you are going to have crazy faith, you cannot waiver or wonder or question. You must tell God

I trust you right now even if I cannot see your hand at work. Then you close your eyes and take a step.

Me - Crazy or Crazy Trust?

The belly of the fish was not a very comfortable place for me. Emotionally I battled with Monday morning blues (and Tuesday through Friday, for that matter). I looked forward to my lunch hour because it was a period when I could be away from my office and create a fantasy for an hour of having a job I enjoyed. As I mentioned previously, the one thing the belly provided was financial security for my family. The biweekly paycheck, company-sponsored health and dental plan, and annual bonus were all things that helped to keep our household afloat financially, or at least I thought. I felt God speaking; He said something like,

> "You are in the belly because you asked to go. Two years ago, I gave you the vision to start your own business, but you ignored me and looked for security. You asked for this dream job, and I gave it to you. I showed you the path to take, but it required a level of faith that you did not have, so you are in the belly. You can only get out of the belly by accepting My plan for your life."

I was terrified. God was calling me to walk away from a successful career into something that did not exist. I was walking into nothing. How could I leave a steady paycheck and all the benefits, no matter how bad the culture was, without a plan? I knew that God spoke to me about His plan two years prior. I even admitted in writing in my journal on August 20, 1999, that I knew His plan before I started this job in 2000. But admitting it and doing it are two very different things.

I struggled with where my career at this company could take me versus knowing that God had a different plan for my life. I spent weeks praying about it, and then one day during prayer time, I got the date that I was to give my two-week notice. If the date stayed with me, there was no risk. So the Lord spoke to my heart and said, "Tell two people so that they can hold you accountable." I e-mailed two friends explaining all God had been saying to me, and I revealed the date of my resignation. It was becoming a reality. I was pondering the riskiest move of my life. If I was wrong about what God was saying to me, I was putting myself and my family at risk of having nothing. That was enough for me to want to call this whole thing off, but I couldn't.

There was still only one income in the house, and God told me to give that up. It did not make sense. In our current financial state, all our bills were always paid on time. Why would God take us into a financially unstable environment? How crazy would it be for me to walk away from a high-paying job when the storm was not over yet? Whenever I thought about changing my mind, God would send confirmation that His decision was correct. One of the most significant confirmations was when I went to my husband in the Spring of 2001 and shared God's plan for my life. My husband said, "If that is what you believe God is calling you to do, then go for it. Am I afraid? Yes. But I support you." Despite my insecurities and quiet doubts, God continued to let me know that He had this one covered.

During the summer of 2001, I attended a family reunion in Charlotte, NC. On Sunday, we attended a church pastored by an old college friend. After service, I went to the bookstore and purchased two tapes of sermons my friend preached. I did not ask for any recommendations. I just looked at the sermon titles and picked two. One was a sermon entitled "What's Going to Happen Next?" It was preached on the first Sunday of 2001 by Bishop Claude R. Alexander, Jr., and confirmed God's call for me to step out on faith. What is the likelihood that a tape I randomly picked up in a bookstore in North Carolina would speak directly to my situation? I would say highly likely when you are dealing with God's divine providence. I did not listen to the message until a month later. At the end of his sermon, Pastor Alexander said, "There's a word over you. There's a word over your life. Step out on faith – start that new business." [10] Because I know that God does not work on coincidence, I knew this word was from God.

Even with the confirmations, the decision was difficult. After deciding in my heart that I would walk in His Word and give my resignation in August, I started receiving counteroffers. I had to stay with the company through my one-year anniversary in September to avoid repaying my sign-on bonus. About three weeks before the date that I decided I would resign, I was called in to see the Chief Financial Officer. I thought maybe they would fire me. This would make the whole process much easier because I would just collect unemployment and maybe even get a little severance package. Not even close! I left the CFO's office with a letter thanking me for my hard work and granting me additional stock benefits. The gain could be substantial if I remained with the company for two more years. With that in mind, you can imagine that the doubts began to creep back into my mind. I mean, if the company thought that much of me to give me these benefits after only one year of service, was I completely sure that God would call me to walk away from that? What better way to honor the Lord than through a successful career?

But He is the same yesterday, today, and forever (Hebrews 13:8). When He told me to start my own business in 1999, He did not change His mind. He was waiting for me to get to that point of dissatisfaction where I would be willing to step out with crazy trust and obey.

---

[10] Bishop Claude R. Alexander is the Pastor of the University Park Baptist Church in Charlotte, NC.

THE STORM: FOR YOUR GOOD AND FOR HIS GLORY

On August 17, 2001 (almost two years to the date I had written in my journal that God confirmed this vision to start my own business), I went to my boss and gave a three-week notice (because I liked him) with a final date of September 7, 2001. While he made resigning difficult because we built a good relationship over the last year, I was focused on doing what God had called me to do despite my fear that I could not be persuaded otherwise. Looking back, I remember focusing on how unhappy I was in my job and how I could not continue to be so stressed out. Now I can see in hindsight that it was not the job causing my unhappiness or my stress; it was about not following God's plan for my life, which was causing the unhappiness and the stress.

On Friday, September 7, 2001, I left my comfortable office and a good-paying job and, with crazy trust, started my own consulting business. I did not look back. Everything I left behind financially was not important. I walked away from a mentality where I believed that the paycheck I earned paid the bills. And I walked into a mentality where I knew that EVERYTHING I received was by His grace and mercy. I walked away from a mentality where I believed that bonuses, salaries, and stock options indicated that you had made it, and I walked into a mentality that declared anything you do that places you outside of God's plan for your life is a waste of time.

I learned the hard way that God had more plans for me than getting up every morning and working at a job just because it provided a paycheck. I had placed God inside a box, and on the outside of the box were written words like stability, bi-weekly paycheck, retirement plan, and security. I was willing to obey as long as God worked within the box where I placed Him. As soon as God pointed outside my box and asked me to break the bi-weekly paycheck mentality, I was terrified. The Lord changed me from the inside out. He delivered me from the belly, not from the storm. Later, I will talk about how deliverance may come from inside first.

I walked out of my job on September 7th, and I walked into my new life. After the terrorist attack on September 11th that destroyed the twin towers, I remember thinking: what if I had been working at this job and something disastrous happened? I would have been sitting at a job I did not enjoy, which may have been the last thing I did. I would never have known the abundant life He had waiting for me in being self-employed.

God was true to His promises. I was able to start a successful business. I loved my work, and my clients were fun. My Provider paid all my bills and took care of my family. By taking that step of crazy trust, He removed that fear of failure. I never marketed my business. My clients all just magically appeared, or better said, divinely appeared. I could not imagine doing anything else, and more importantly, I was at peace because I was on His plan.

Do You Have Crazy Trust?

What about you? Is something pressing in your spirit that seems just too crazy to be God? Is there something that you feel God is speaking to you about that is against anything you might believe is logical from a human perspective? Are you wondering whether God is calling you to step into nothing and exhibit crazy trust? If your answer to any of these questions is "yes," then it's time for you to seek God's face and find the answer. The important thing about crazy trust is that if you are stepping out onto or into your fabrication of God's message to you, then you will just be crazy. You must know that the illogical step you are about to take is God and not you. Sometimes that is easier said than done.

If you are like me, it is easy to conclude that such an illogical move as leaving a comfortable job with a stable, regular biweekly paycheck certainly can't be a message from God because it's too crazy, so it must be the devil. Don't be too quick to assume it is the devil. The scripture says in Psalm 37:4 – *"Delight yourself in the Lord, and He will give you the desires of your heart."* God knew that it was my heart's desire to run my own business. He also knew that I was afraid of trying and failing. It was not a crazy thought that I would run my own business; what was crazy was how God was calling me to do it. However, God often asks us to do what seems illogical from a human perspective to accomplish His will. We have looked at three examples of this already: Noah, Abraham, and Gideon.

Because it is important to know that God may call you to do something that defies human logic, you must be connected to the Source. You must invest significant time talking with God about what is in your heart. Ask Him for confirmation, and then ask Him for confirmation again. If it is something God is calling you to do, the call will not change. If He places it in your heart, He will continue to place it in your heart. I have often heard the question: how can I be sure it is God? The answer is that He will confirm it, which results in an overwhelming sense of peace. Philippians 4:6 -7 states, *"Do not be anxious about anything, but in everything, by prayer and petition, with thanksgiving, present your requests to God. And the peace of God, which transcends all understanding, will guard your hearts and your minds in Christ Jesus."*

God will reveal His will for your life and tell you if there is some crazy trust you must exhibit, but you must pray, listen, and seek Him. When I say listen, I mean listen to the Spirit of God. You must be careful about listening to others when talking about crazy trust. People will tell you that you are wrong and taking a big risk. Your best friend might not support you, and your mother might question it. But you must hear from God on this: once God says it, that is all you need to hear. You do not need anyone else to validate a word that God has given you.

But allow me to extend one piece of personal advice if your step of faith involves your financial situation, and you are not a tither, press pause. This book is not on tithing, but as one who can testify that obedience to the Word for giving pleases God, I believe that many of our financial struggles are directly related to how we handle God's money. Malachi 3:9-10 states, *"You are under a curse – the whole nation of you – because you are robbing me. Bring the whole tithe into the storehouse, that there may be food in my house. 'Test me in this,' says the Lord Almighty, 'and see if I will not throw open the floodgates of heaven and pour out so much blessing that you will not have room enough for it.'"* If your calling is like mine and requires you to move from financial security (from human standards) into financial nothingness, you must make sure that under your financial nothingness is Christ, the solid rock. You don't want to find yourself at the beginning of a storm resulting because you are robbing God.

When we were a two-income household, we tithed and gave offerings without much concern about lacking finances. When we became a one-income household, and the income did not always appear to cover the expenses, we tithed and gave an offering, and He provided the difference. As I am sure many tithers will agree, in the beginning, you are afraid to tithe, but once you become a committed tither, you are afraid <u>not</u> to tithe.

For some of you, tithing may be your step toward crazy trust. Maybe your income falls short of your expenses on paper, and God is pressing in your spirit to tithe. By human logic, it does not make sense. Your budget may indicate that you need $100 more each month to pay your bills, and, as a result, there is always one bill that does not get paid. God is calling you to tithe 10% of your income, which would mean $333 per month based on your salary. Now clearly, the math does not work in this situation. Your budget shortfall would increase from $100 each month to $433. Why would God call you to make such a financially irresponsible move? He wants you to trust him to make up the $433 shortage plus more. He wants to prove Himself.

Step Out of the Boat

One of our biggest problems as Christians is that we talk a good religious game, but when it comes to playing ball, we fall short. Peter is known for this type of big talk in the gospels. You can often find Peter running off at the mouth before thinking much about what he is saying. In Matthew 14:22-33, we find the disciples in a boat as Jesus is left on shore to dismiss the crowd. Jesus begins to walk on top of the water toward the disciples out in the boat. When the disciples see Jesus approaching, they are afraid and assume it is a ghost. Jesus identifies Himself to them, and Peter feels the need to tell Jesus, "Prove it." When Jesus calls Peter to come out to Him on the water, Peter boldly steps out and starts to walk toward Him. As the winds and the waves blow, Peter begins to get afraid and starts sinking. You may have heard it preached or taught that we begin to sink when we take our eyes off Jesus and focus on the winds and waves of life. This lesson rings particularly true when you are in a storm. It is critical to keep your eyes focused not on yourself or your situation but on Jesus, who can and will deliver you in His time.

But there is another important lesson to identify from this story that specifically relates to crazy trust. When Jesus called Peter out onto the water, Peter was in the boat. Jesus, however, was not in the boat. Some of us are in the boat calling Jesus to get in with us. Jesus calls us out of the boat to follow Him where He wants us to go. We need to stop and recognize that Jesus is not in the boat.[11] Unlike Peter, we are not even willing to step out of the boat to walk to Jesus because we are too afraid that we will sink. We believe that in the boat, we are safe from drowning; however, we often miss the pinhole in the bottom of the boat and are unaware that the boat is taking on water.

---

[11] Thought credited to Rev. John M. Borders, III, Pastor of Morning Star Baptist Church in Mattapan, MA from a sermon entitled "Death of an Illusion."

Most of the disciples were fishermen, so the boat was a very comfortable place. For us, our boat is wherever we are comfortable. God calls us out of our comfort zone and into His plan for our lives. I don't mean to imply any particular sin associated with staying in your boat because there may not be. But if God is trying to take your life in another direction or, as John 10:10 says, "give you life more abundantly," and you refuse to leave your boat, you might be missing the blessing. You might settle for mediocrity because you will not trust God enough to get out of the boat and walk on water. Everyone is not meant to be a great preacher, evangelist, author, or corporate executive, but if you ask any successful person, they will tell you that some risks were required to get to where they are now. When you know that God is calling you, it's a calculated risk where the guarantor is already in place. Since God already has the answer, you don't have to worry about the outcome; you only must be obedient to Him and trust Him.

It took two years of prayer, wrestling, and insecurity, along with one year in the belly of my own fish, before I was ready to trust God in a crazy way. I pray that you do not shut out that pressing feeling in your spirit that you should be doing something else just because it does not seem logical. Isaiah 55:8 reminds us, "*For my thoughts are not your thoughts, neither are your ways my ways, declares the Lord.*" While we might be able to come up with the ideal circumstances under which taking a certain path may be acceptable, God will often design a much more complex path. He wants to make sure that you are committed to His plan and wants you to make sacrifices to get there. He wants you to trust Him like crazy.

Chapter 8

Deliverance May Come Inside First

Matthew 5:44 – *"But I tell you: Love your enemies and pray for those who persecute you."*

2 Chronicles 20:15(b) – *"Do not be afraid or discouraged because of this vast army. For the battle is not yours, but God's."*

If you have ever been in a strong storm, you have undoubtedly heard the phrase "God will deliver you" more than once. I heard it much more than I cared to during my storm. You can get to the point where you want to say to the next person, "Well, if you are so sure, then tell me when." The frustration of a storm is that you do not know when it will end, and it always seems to last longer than you believe you can endure. However, when we think of deliverance from the storm, we think of the storm ending, and therefore we are delivered. But sometimes, God will deliver us mentally and emotionally, and then the storm will cease.

It is a lot easier to weather the storm when you have been delivered inside first. The three Hebrew boys (Shadrach, Meshach, and Abednego) that were thrown into the fiery furnace in Daniel 3 were emotionally and mentally free before they even entered the storm of the fiery furnace. Because they refused to bow down and worship the image of gold that King Nebuchadnezzar had set up, they were to be thrown into a fiery furnace. When the King challenged them as to whether their God could rescue them from his hand, they responded, *"O Nebuchadnezzar, we do not need to defend ourselves before you in this matter. If we are thrown into the blazing furnace, the God we serve is able to save us from it, and he will rescue us from your hand, O king. But even if he does not, we want you to know, O King, that we will not serve your gods or worship the image of gold you have set up"* (Daniel 3:16-18). The Hebrew boys were not concerned about the outcome of their storm, they were not concerned about the conditions of their storm, and they were not focused on deliverance from their storm. They were already delivered because they knew who was controlling the storm.

The king thought he controlled the storm, but the Hebrew boys knew differently. They knew that NOTHING was about to happen that God did not already have covered. It would have been easy for the Hebrew boys to spend their energy exhibiting anger toward the men who snitched to the king that they were not worshipping his golden image. They might have spent energy discussing how unfair the king's punishment was or how evil the king was for not showing mercy to them. They could have agonized over how hot the furnace would be, how badly they might be burned, or how slowly they might die. But none of those things preoccupied their minds. Shadrach, Meshach and Abednego were clear on who God was, what He could do, and how worthy He was of everything they counted valuable, including their lives.

What Is Inside Deliverance?

Inside deliverance happens when God delivers you on the inside - there is no lightning flash but a peace that passes all understanding. When God delivers you from the inside, you will feel like Jesus did in Mark 4:35-41 when He was sleeping in the stern of the boat while a fierce storm raged around it. The disciples awakened Jesus in a panicked state, exclaiming, *"Master, carest Thou not that we perish?"* (Mark 4:38 KJV). It was not that Jesus was unaware of the storm swirling around them; He knew there was a storm, but He also knew who was in control of the storm. When you are delivered from the inside, you know there is a storm, and you realize WHO is in control of the storm.

When we are in the drowning stage, we unconsciously believe that satan is controlling the storm. We begin to believe that because satan continues to attack from all angles, he is controlling things. Sometimes I wonder if satan thinks he is controlling things as well. But the reality is that satan is only allowed to go as far as God will allow him. In the story of Job, satan had to get permission from God to touch Job's possessions. Then he had to get permission to afflict Job's body. Satan wanted to kill Job and was hoping Job would kill himself since God did not give satan permission to take Job's life.

Deliverance from the inside does not come by osmosis. Your deliverance requires some action and effort on your part. You cannot expect that because you ask God to deliver you each night before you fall asleep *during* your prayer in your bed, you will get results. Deliverance requires a level of desperation. The Synoptic Gospels (Matthew, Mark, and Luke) are full of stories of desperate people seeking Jesus to be delivered from something, be it sickness, demons, death, or whatever. These people knew what power Jesus had, and they took desperate measures to reach Him. We addressed two of these examples in chapter 6, where we discussed the desperation that comes from being in the belly. Remember, you must combine faith with desperation. You cannot just be desperate for God's deliverance - you must believe He can deliver you. The first response of the Hebrew boys in the book of Daniel was that God was able to deliver them.

If you do not believe that God can deliver you, then you are not likely to be delivered until you do. Hebrews 11:1 states, *"faith is the substance of things hoped for, the evidence of things not seen"* (KJV). When the clouds in the storm are still dark, the wind is still swirling around you, and there seems to be no end in sight, you must trust that God is a deliverer. It is more than just saying the religious phrase, "God will deliver you." The comfort is knowing that God is ABLE to deliver you even if He does not deliver you when you believe He should. Faith means continuing to believe that God is in control well after your human mind tells you that you should have been delivered already.

My Inside Delivery

I could not predict when my storm would end, nor did I know why it was still raging, and there was not much I could do to make it stop. I could not do anything to move the process along more quickly. Therefore, as one would do to prepare for a hurricane, I had to board up my house and get ready for the unpredictable. I had been through the pity party stage, the drowning stage, and the treading water stage. Then I started swimming. But to where was I swimming? The storm was still raging, and although I was in better shape mentally and spiritually to handle it, I still had no direction. Without direction, it is easy to get pulled along with the tide, but I had come too far to be a part of that tide. The tide would only take me back to the drowning stage.

I fought against the tide of my storm with the weapon of prayer. I began to pray for those very people who created the lie and prayed for the salvation of those who caused or perpetuated the circumstances of my storm. Admittedly, at first, my prayers were out of obligation. Jesus commands us in Matthew 5:44 to love our enemies and pray for those who persecute us. So, in obedience to His command, I was praying for my enemies. But the sincerity behind prayer is more important than the prayer itself.

At first, I would just pray a generic prayer that God would help me not hate the creators of the lies and that He would make them recognize Him and repent. However, my desire for them to repent was not so that they would find the Savior but that they would simply disappear. Ultimately, the prayer was more about me than about them. Once, during an intense moment between the Father and me, I explained to the Lord that I was trying to pray for them, but the reality was that in my heart, I wished some harm to them the way they caused harm to me. In those moments, the Holy Spirit spoke deep into my spirit. His words sounded something like this:

> *I know that you are unhappy. I know you are angry because some are plotting against you and yours. I do feel your pain. But you must recognize and believe that your battle is not against flesh and blood (Ephesians 6:12), though you have behaved as if that were the case. More importantly, you have allowed the devil to use anger to block you from witnessing about Me to the world. Did you forget that you are the salt of the earth (Matthew 5:13)? Did you forget that you are to let your light shine before men, that they may see your good deeds and praise Me (Matthew 5:16)? You have made this whole thing about you. What about Me? You are the only Bible that some people will ever read; how do you read right now? I need you to represent me. I need people to look at you and see the grace of God. I need you to believe that you do not need revenge because My grace is sufficient for you (2 Corinthians 12:9). I need you to turn this around and use it for My glory.*

It was that one encounter with the Holy Spirit that changed my perspective. From then on, I found myself praying for those same people who perpetuate lies with a concern that only Jesus could give me. I prayed for their salvation because it was clear they were lost. I did not need revenge any longer. I already had one up on them because I had Jesus.

It was not just prayer that gave me inside deliverance. The conversation with the Father told Him how I felt because I knew my heart was not right. I had to admit to God that I was not in full compliance with His Word and was only going through the motions. God saw fit to send His Spirit down for a personal conversation with me. That personal conversation, summarized above, was based on His Word. Scripture was the second weapon that I used for my deliverance.

Once I felt free from anger and unhealthy attitudes toward others, I used the promises in God's Word as a stepping stone. It is easier to be humble and take on the spirit of Christ, which to some appears weak and wimpish when you know what His Word says. The carnal mind thinks strength has to do with how forcefully we respond to something or someone. The spiritual mind knows that strength is not how forcefully but how Christ-like you respond. How we respond in any given situation must be based on the Word of God. The Beatitudes in Matthew 5 are a perfect example of what is blessed by the Word of God would be considered a weakness by the world. In verses 3-11 of that chapter, Jesus provides a list of people who will be blessed:

- the poor in spirit
- those who mourn
- the meek
- those who hunger and thirst for righteousness
- the merciful
- the pure in heart
- the peacemakers

- those who are persecuted
- those who insult, persecute you and falsely say all kinds of evil against you because of Christ.

The world would look at this list and say it is the equivalent of saying, "Blessed are those of you who are weak." We cannot live by the world's standards. The world says you are blessed when you go out and do what it takes to get your blessing. The Lord says I will bless you because you are my child and follow my commands. Jesus closes out this section on the Beatitudes with verse 12, saying, *"Rejoice and be glad, because great is your reward in heaven, for, in the same way, they persecuted the prophets who were before you."* We must stand on the promise that our rewards will not all be material blessings here on earth; some of our rewards will be in heaven.

The Word of God serves as a solid foundation upon which we can stand, knowing in our hearts and minds that no matter what is going on outside of us, inside, there is peace. You have peace when you can claim:

- **"No weapon formed against thee shall prosper"** (Isaiah 54:17 KJV);
- **"No, in all these things we are more than conquerors through him who loved us"** (Romans 8:37);
- **"Being confident of this, that he who began a good work in you will carry it on to completion until the day of Christ Jesus"** (Philippians 1:6);
- **"In all things God works for the good of those who love him, who have been called according to his purpose"** (Romans 8:28);
- **"For I have learned to be content whatever the circumstances"** (Philippians 4:11);
- **I can do everything through him who gives me strength** (Philippians 4:13).

Peace comes from not only knowing the Word but also believing it and recognizing that whatever storms you are in or battling against, the God who created the universe is leading the battle. In 2 Chronicles chapter 20, Jehoshaphat faces the reality that a vast army is coming from Edom to fight against him. Realizing that he is outnumbered, Jehoshaphat seeks the Lord in front of all of Judah. When Jehoshaphat seeks God, he gets the answer to his dilemma: ***"Do not be afraid or discouraged because of this vast army. For the battle is not yours, but God's"*** (verse 15). What a great confirmation to have God communicate that the battle is His. Who better to handle a battle where the odds are against you? I don't know about you, but there is no one else I would rather have fighting my battle.

The final weapons for my internal deliverance were praise and worship. I learned that praise and worship put a nice sealant coat over the wall of prayer and the Word of God. We each have our own style of praise. Some of us are quiet, maybe with an "amen" or a wave, and some shout out a hearty "hallelujah." I am from both schools. While I fully agree that you do not have to jump and shout for God to know that you appreciate Him, I believe there are times in your storm when you need to get out of *your* box and give God unrestricted praise like David in 2 Samuel 6:14. I was consistently in the quiet camp for the first 20 years of my Christian life. In the past, when the Spirit hit me, I might cry (and that still happens), but amid searching for deliverance, I discovered that I found an overwhelming peace whenever I pulled out my "alabaster box praise."

There is a story in Matthew 26 that describes a woman who came to Jesus and poured an alabaster box of expensive perfume over Jesus' head. She then began to wash his feet with her tears and dry them with her hair. This woman forgot about protocol, ignored customs and traditions, disregarded how dirty her hair would be when she finished and did not care how much her perfume cost her. She was desperate for Jesus.

Whether in the privacy of my bedroom or in a public setting, I found that when I release everything in me to the glory of God, there comes that peace that passes all understanding. When you get to that desperate point in your storm where you want Jesus bad enough not to care what anyone else thinks, you too will open an "alabaster box praise" and worship Him until you find that peace. Do not wait 20 years, as I did, to find out that praise and worship are awesome weapons against the devil. There is an element of truth to the popular cliché: "Deliverance is in your praise."

Chapter 9

And It Can Get Worse

Psalm 73:2-3 – *"But as for me, my feet had almost slipped; I had nearly lost my foothold. For I envied the arrogant when I saw the prosperity of the wicked."*

Exodus 14:4 – *"And I will harden Pharaoh's heart, and he will pursue them. But I will gain glory for myself through Pharaoh and all his army, and the Egyptians will know that I am the Lord."*

The feeling of deliverance on the inside is wonderful and makes you see the world in a whole new light. However, deliverance inside does not translate to deliverance from your circumstances. You may be delivered on the inside yet still be in the middle of a storm. It is quite possible that things could get worse after you are delivered on the inside.

Inside deliverance can be as simple as recognizing that God is in control of your situation, gaining new praise in your spirit, and becoming a daily student of the Word. Perhaps three weeks after your inside deliverance, you still do not have a new job, and the mortgage is due. In this instance, your attitude may have changed, but your circumstances have not. This imbalance between inside and outside deliverance can easily result in discouragement, disillusionment, and a return to the drowning phase if you do not actively continue to use the weapons that delivered you on the inside.

Look again at the story of Job: First, Job lost his donkeys and the servants who were plowing the fields. Next, he lost his sheep and the servants tending those sheep. Then, he lost his camels and the servants who were with those camels. As if that is not enough, he lost all ten of his children because a mighty wind caused his house to collapse. In the blink of an eye, Job lost what was important to him in one day: his animals, servants, and children.

Without a doubt, Job's circumstances put him in a storm. However, Job's response in Job 1:21 is remarkable and one that we can all take a lesson from: *"**Naked I came out of my mother's womb, and naked I shall return thither: the Lord gave and the Lord hath taken away; blessed be the name of the Lord**"* (KJV). This response showed Job's complete deliverance on the inside. Job was not moved by satan's attempt to get him to sin. In verses 9-11, satan states that Job serves the Lord because of all that God has given him and that if all these blessings were removed, Job would not be so faithful. So why did things get worse if Job stood the test and did not allow the devil's scheme to succeed because he was delivered on the inside?

As if the loss of animals, servants, and children were not enough, Job also lost his health. Job was still a faithful servant, still blameless and upright in the eyes of God, yet he was inflicted with painful sores from head to toe. When you look at the first half of the story, you might conclude that Job passed the test, so the storm should be over, but that is not the case here. Job did pass the test, but it got worse when it should have gotten better.

As the story continues, Job's wife and friends begin to question what Job had done to deserve such continual winds and waves in his life. The human mind can only comprehend that this type of punishment from God must result from disobedient or displeasing behavior. However, this was not the case with Job. The story begins with God clearly stating, *"Have you considered my servant Job? There is no one on earth like him; he is blameless and upright, a man who fears God and shuns evil"* (Job 1:8). What a compliment to have God tell the devil you are upright and blameless. With that in mind, why did God allow Job to be put through such a storm by the devil? And after passing the first test, why did God allow Job's situation to get worse?

Simply stated, God chooses whom he uses. God chose to use Job. Job did not ask to be used; he was chosen. It is an honor to be chosen, but being chosen can bring hardship and heartache. Being chosen by God means that sometimes things you do not and will not understand will happen. It means that God's glory will be seen through your life. For God's glory to be seen through you or me, cleaning and purging must occur.

Job understood the process of being cleansed and used by God in Job 23:10: *"But he knows the way that I take; when he has tested me, I will come forth as gold."* We all know the analogy of making gold; it must be placed in the fire so that all the impurities are burned out. That is what getting worse is all about. While we often think we have passed the test because we have reached a certain level of growth or understanding, God has not finished making, cleaning, and shining us up for His glory. The first test might have only made us and cleaned us, but we may be a little dull from the dust of the fire, so God may allow things to get a little bit worse so that he can add that shine. Gold is worth a lot, and part of the value is what it takes to make gold pure. Much of the value of our testimony for God is in what it took for Him to make us into whom we have become for Him.

The Limbo State

When you reach the level of growth where you have deliverance on the inside, you may feel like you are in a state of limbo because the circumstances on the outside have not changed. You begin to feel like God is taking a siesta. With your newfound peace of mind, you are ready to move and shake the world; you are ready for whatever assignment God has for you (or so you think). You cannot understand why God is not moving in your life. You look at how far God has brought you spiritually, and you think that God has done all of this for a reason. Now you are ready to put things into action. But God does not seem to be doing anything; you are in limbo.

The limbo state can be dangerous because it tends to produce a sense of frustration. In our humanity, we can get frustrated with God when things are not moving according to our plan. The danger in this frustration is how we handle it. We can 1) mistakenly take matters into our own hands and begin to move in areas that are of our choosing or make decisions without God, 2) begin to slip back into the state of worry and concern about why God is not acting on or reacting to our requests, pleas, and demands, or 3) remain in our state of internal deliverance knowing that despite His appearance of silence, He is still at work in our life and our situation. The first two options can delay our ultimate deliverance because they are contrary to God's will.

The limbo state is our interpretation of the situation because the reality is that God is and has been working the entire time. He is not in limbo; He knows what He is doing and has the timing perfected. Our frustration is that He has not consulted with us or informed us of His entire plan. But the Lord makes it clear in Isaiah 55:8 that we aren't on His level, "***For my thoughts are not your thoughts, neither are your ways my ways.***" We cannot comprehend what God is thinking or planning; therefore, the third option of remaining in our state of internal deliverance is the best.

We must reconcile ourselves to the reality that He is in charge, and He controls the strategic plan. Our job is to trust God to know what is best for us. *"And we know that in all things God works for the good of those who love him, who have been called according to his purpose"* (Romans 8:28).

What Is Worse?

The idea that things can get worse automatically implies a comparison – worse than what? If God is in control at the beginning, and God is in control in the middle, then how can it get worse? What event could occur to make things worse? It's all a matter of perspective; no matter what happens between the beginning of your storm and the point that things appear to get worse, the following remains true:

- *"Jesus Christ is the same yesterday and today and forever"* (Hebrews 13:8);
- For He knows the plans He has for you, plans to prosper you and not to harm you, and plans to give you hope and a future (Jeremiah 29:11 paraphrased);
- His grace is sufficient for you (2 Corinthians 12:9 paraphrased);
- God will supply all your needs according to his riches in glory (Philippians 4:19 paraphrased).

The bottom line is that the Word of God remains true, and if we believe and stand on this Word, no matter what happens in our circumstances, our perspective should not change.

Our circumstances can worsen, but only when we allow our perspective to change. When we look through our eyes, we see the changing circumstances as threatening our ability to survive. Worry and doubt begin to creep in and consume our thinking until we allow our perspective to be governed by the words of the apostle Paul in Philippians 4:11-12, *"I am not saying this because I am in need, for I have learned to be content whatever the circumstances. I know what it is to be in need, and I know what it is to have plenty. I have learned the secret of being content in any and every situation."* If you have not learned the secret of being content in any and every situation, then it is time that you did, and if you know the secret, then it is time to put it into practice.

Chapter 10

It's All for His Glory

Psalm 115:3 – *"**Our God is in heaven; He does whatever pleases Him.**"*

In our limited knowledge and thinking, we look at the storms in our life and wonder how a God who loves us could allow us to go through tough times. We have the mistaken impression that God is like Santa Claus and His job is to give us gifts and make us happy. We like to quote all the passages of scripture that portray God as the giver and the blesser who is making a list of all the things we need. We are biased toward passages like James 4:2(b): *"**You do not have because you do not ask.**"* We like the idea of being able to go to God and ask for what we need or want, but we do not like it when God requires something of us in return.

Whether God is allowing us to go through a storm or has designed the storm Himself, the intention of the storm remains the same – it is for your good and for His glory. At the beginning of the world, God created man in His image. He could have created man in the image of another animal, but He created man in His image because it would glorify Him. Humans were designed to be a direct manifestation of God, and man's purpose is to glorify God. Everything that brings glory to God will not always be something we enjoy. This is not to imply that God takes pleasure in circumstances or events that make us unhappy, but sacrifice is required so that He might be glorified. For most of us, sacrifice is a difficult and unpleasant experience.

For Your Good, Not Your Pleasure

As a child, I remember hearing the phrase, "It's for your own good." This phrase never seemed to be associated with something enjoyable. For example, I have never been particularly fond of vegetables; as a matter of fact, I only like four. I remember my mother telling me that I needed to eat my vegetables because they were good for me, but I will never like peas or cooked carrots, no matter how good they are for me.

The same can be true for the storms in our lives. No matter how good the storm is for you spiritually, you will not like it. No matter how good it is for you, it may still be very painful. The storm can be likened to pottery. It begins as a lump of clay with no form or definition, and the potter molds it into art. As the potter works his magic, you can begin to see the clay form into something recognizable. After the potter forms the clay into a pot, it looks good to the naked eye, but it is not complete. The pot is completed by placing it in a kiln (oven) and baking it at a high temperature. In the kiln, the pottery is baked at such a high temperature that all the impurities are burned out. When it is complete, the piece of pottery not only looks good but is also solidified, bonded, and made as close to perfect as possible. In the final step, the pottery is painted or glazed to provide that glossy finish.

The process of making us into Christ-like beings is similar. We start as lumps of clay that Christ begins to mold. The molding process can be painful, but when we get into the kilns of life, we feel the pain of burning out our impurities. We must adopt the "Job attitude" when the heat of our storm becomes the temperature of the kiln: "***But he knows the way that I take; when he has tested me, I will come forth as gold***" (Job 23:10).

You may have heard sermons or advice telling you that life's trials and storms build, clean, and make us more like Christ. As one who has been in the storm, I can tell you that this information does not help – until you understand and accept that the storm around you is no longer controlling you. When you have learned to swim and not drown, when you have been broken and made whole, and when you have been delivered from the inside, then you can understand that the storm is for your good, and you will begin to see all the changes that have taken place inside you.

It will be difficult to get to the point James calls us to when he tells us to "count it all joy," but you will find yourself in agreement with his conclusion of what the test has done and will do for you.

> "***Consider it pure joy, my brothers, whenever you face trials of many kinds because you know that the testing of your faith develops perseverance. Perseverance must finish its work so that you may be mature and complete, not lacking anything***" (James 1:2-4).

The final message from James is clear: to be mature and complete, lacking nothing, you will face trials of many kinds. Some things in our lives require a storm for us to recognize them, get rid of them, or fix them. Because God is sovereign, He knows that some lessons will be painful for us to learn.

Be of good courage because James tells us, "***Blessed is the man who perseveres under trial, because when he has stood the test, he will receive the crown of life that God has promised to those who love him***" (James 1:12). With that promise as a backdrop, persevering through a storm becomes a bit easier. The storm may not be any less painful, but recognizing that there is a promise of blessing and a crown of life at the end can ease the pain.

One of the most familiar passages of scripture that Christians quote in times of difficulty is Romans 8:28: *"And we know that in all things God works for the good of those who love him, who have been called according to his purpose."* Sometimes in quoting this passage, we forget that there are two conditions on this promise: 1) it is for those who love Him, and 2) it is for those called according to His purpose. The first condition requires us to love Him. We all like to say we love the Lord as a matter of "religiosity"; however, in John 14:15, Jesus tells us how we prove that we love Him: *"if you love me, you will obey what I command."* The commands of Christ are clearly outlined in His Word. You cannot question whether He is working it out for your good if you are not living up to the first condition of loving Him and obeying His commands.

The second condition is that we be called according to His purpose. Many of us are within God's general will because we have accepted Him as our personal Savior and Lord, but we are not walking in His specific purpose for our life. Many of us are aware of God's callings for us in various parts of the ministry, but we are not walking in those callings for various reasons. Standing on the promise of Romans 8:28 means we must be committed to loving Him and have accepted His call and will for our life. Some people are not clear about what God's will for their life is or what His specific call is. That is another book in itself, but, in short, I will say that if you seek God for His will, and I mean earnestly seek Him, He will reveal it to you.

It may not seem like it's for your good, and you may have difficulty getting to the point where you are joyful that you have encountered the trial, but if you reach the point where you realize that it has all been for your good, you will be pleased with how the storm has changed you. You can look back at where God has brought you from, how He has changed you, and where He has moved you, and you can be grateful that the storm did not last forever. You can be grateful that it did not kill you and that God kept you on His mind. You will know that the storm and all its pain and struggle have been for your good.

Temporary Sacrifice for His Glory

In the gospel of John, chapter 11, we find that Jesus had received word that Lazarus was sick. It is important to identify who Lazarus was to Jesus. He was not a stranger or just another desperate person looking for healing; Lazarus was the brother of Mary and Martha. Mary and Martha invited Jesus into their home (Luke 10), and while Martha was working diligently, Mary was sitting at Jesus' feet.

The scripture states in John 11:5-6: *"**Jesus loved Martha and her sister and Lazarus. Yet when he heard that Lazarus was sick, he stayed where he was two more days.**"* It seems illogical that Jesus loved Lazarus, yet he stayed where He was for two more days when He heard of his illness. Jesus had healed many that He did not know with just one touch, yet someone He loved was ill, and he did not rush to Lazarus. Jesus gave us the conclusion of this story in John 11:4: *"**This sickness will not end in death. No, it is for God's glory so that God's Son may be glorified through it.**"*

When Jesus arrived in Bethany, Lazarus had already been in a tomb for four days. From a clinical perspective, Lazarus' body had begun to decay, and rigor mortis had likely set in, given there was no embalming process as we have today. The fact that Lazarus was already dead when Jesus arrived must have puzzled the disciples, as it would you or I. Jesus had just declared to them that Lazarus' illness would not result in death, yet now he was dead. But that's typical of Jesus. He likes to operate when the odds are against Him so that He can confirm his power.

When Martha heard that Jesus had finally arrived, she went to meet Him. I can imagine that Martha was not too happy with

Jesus. In verse 21, Martha says to Jesus, *"**Lord, if you had been here, my brother would not have died.**"* To put it quite plainly, Martha blamed Jesus for Lazarus' death because she knew Jesus had the power to heal Lazarus. But despite Martha's frustration or anger toward Jesus for His delay, she recognized this was still Jesus. In verse 22, she followed her accusation with a statement of belief, *"**But I know that even now God will give you whatever you ask.**"*

Jesus continued to set the stage for God to receive all the glory. Mary came out to meet Him and uttered the same accusation as Martha - that Lazarus would not have died if Jesus had been present. He was deeply moved by her grief and wept. Before calling Lazarus from the dead, He spoke to Mary, Martha, and all those gathered in mourning, *"**Did I not tell you that if you believed, you would see the glory of God?**"* (John 11:40).

Lazarus' death proved that nothing is impossible for God. Dead for four days, with a stench from the tomb and wrapped in grave clothes, Lazarus walked out of the tomb. Jesus' ultimate lesson was to teach that the power of God is limitless. Lazarus had to die, and his sisters had to go through days of mourning so that God might be glorified by Lazarus' return. It was not about Mary and Martha, their grief, or preferential treatment for their relationship with Jesus, and it wasn't even about Lazarus. It was about showing those present that Jesus was the Son of the Living God. In John 41-42, Jesus explains why this incident needed to be so dramatic: *"**Father, I thank you that you have heard me. I knew that you always hear me, but I said this for the benefit of the people standing here, that they may believe that you sent me.**"*

The death of Lazarus was Mary's and Martha's storm. Anyone who has lost a close loved one will agree that although death is natural and imminent, the emotional toll it can take on you is a storm (we'll revisit this in a later chapter). For some, it is a rainstorm that lasts only briefly; for others, it is more like a hurricane that seems to last forever. God used this storm for His glory.

Permanent Sacrifice for His Glory

Look for a moment at the ultimate sacrifice. When you look around today, you see some men and women of God with awesome ministries that reach thousands of people each year. However, none can compare to Jesus' ministry when He walked this earth. He gave His life as the ultimate sacrifice so that God might be glorified. Jesus' death on the cross was gruesome, painful, and shameful. Crucifixion must be the cruelest and most painful way that anyone could die. The gospel of John provides the most detailed description of the death of Christ, but because crucifixion was so common in that day, all the gory details are not recorded. After researching the process of crucifixion and combining that with the sequence in the gospels, the following is my layperson's summary of the ultimate sacrifice:

> Jesus was arrested at Gethsemane and brought before the high priest for questioning. The guards blindfolded Jesus and spat on Him. As the high priest questioned Him, He was struck in the face for giving what they thought was the wrong answer. The guards continued to taunt Jesus, spitting on Him and striking him in the face as they passed by. Jesus was found guilty of blasphemy.
>
> The next morning, battered, bruised, dehydrated, and exhausted from a sleepless night, Jesus was brought before Pontius Pilate to be charged and sentenced because only the Romans had permission to execute. Pilate found no charges to bring and sent Jesus to Herod. Herod found no crime and sent Him back to Pilate. Pilate wanted to release Jesus, but the crowd shouted, "Crucify

Him!" With pressure from the crowd, Pilate condemned Jesus to flogging and crucifixion.

In preparation for flogging, Jesus was stripped of His clothing, and his hands were tied to a post above his head. A Roman guard stepped forward with a flagellum (short whip) and brought it down with full force against Jesus' shoulders, back, and legs. Over and over, the guard beat Jesus until the whip cut through His skin and deep into the tissue. Blood oozed from His veins. The skin of His back hung like long ribbons, and the entire area was an unrecognizable mass of blood. Ancient Jewish law prohibited more than 40 lashes, but it is doubtful that the Romans adhered to Jewish law.

Finally, the barely-conscious Jesus was untied and allowed to slump to the ground in His blood. The Roman soldiers thought this was a joke. They put a robe on Jesus and placed a stick in his hand for a scepter. They placed a crown of thorns on His head and pressed it into His scalp. Because the scalp is one of the most vascular areas of the body, blood streamed down Jesus' head as the thorns dug in. The Roman soldiers began to taunt Jesus saying, "All hail the king," while laughing. They took the stick from His hand and beat Him over the head, which drove the thorns in deeper. To top off this sadistic game, they ripped the robe from His back, which by this time had begun to stick to the open wounds from the flogging, tearing His skin even more. The excruciating pain caused Jesus to cringe.

Isaiah 52:14 records the prophesy that Jesus was beaten so badly he could not be recognized, and no one wanted to look at Him.

The intense pain and blood loss likely left Jesus in a pre-shock state. Even before the actual crucifixion, Jesus' physical condition was serious, if not critical.

When the soldiers had enough sadistic fun, Jesus was given back his clothing, and the heavy crossbar was placed across his shoulders. The condemned only carried the crossbar, as the upright was permanently in the ground. The procession of the condemned Christ, two thieves, and the Roman soldiers began the slow 650-yard journey. The weight of the crossbar was anywhere from 75–125 lbs. In the condition Jesus was in, He could not carry it. He stumbled and fell, so the soldiers tapped Simon of Cyrene to carry the cross.

As they entered the execution site, Jesus was offered a drink of wine, but He refused. This bitter drink was offered to victims to help numb the pain of crucifixion. The soldiers ordered Simon to drop the crossbar and threw Jesus to the ground with His shoulders pressed against the wood. A Roman soldier felt for the depression in the front of Jesus' wrist and drove the nail into the center. The soldier moved to His other side and nailed His other wrist to the crossbar. The nails were not driven into Jesus' hands because the palms would not support the weight of the body, but by driving the nail into the center of the wrist, there was no injury to a major artery or fracture of any bones.

Jesus' feet were nailed to the cross by placing the left foot against the right foot, and with both feet extended, the nail was driven through each arch. His knees were left moderately flexed. As Jesus hung crucified, his weight began to pull on the nails in his wrists, causing excruciating pain. As He used his feet to push Himself upward to avoid the stretching torment, He placed His full weight on the nail through His feet. He experienced unbearable agony as the nail tore through the nerves between the bones of the feet.

Jesus' arms were fatigued at this point, and cramps swept over His muscles, knotting them in deep, relentless, throbbing pain. These cramps made it difficult for Jesus to push Himself upward. Jesus began to fight for breath. He fought to raise Himself to get a short breath. Each time Jesus brought Himself up for a short breath, He uttered one of the seven last words recorded in scripture.

While Jesus struggled for life, the Roman soldiers threw dice for his garments. Jesus uttered, *"Forgive them, Father, for they know not what they do"* (Luke 23:34 KJV).

As Jesus neared death, He cried, *"My God, my God, why hast thou forsaken me"* (Mark 15:34 KJV). You see, God is too holy for sin, so as Jesus bore the sins of the world, God the Father had to turn from His son.

After hours of unrelenting pain, extensive loss of blood, and the shame of the world's sins on His shoulders, Jesus uttered a few additional phrases and said, *"It is finished"* (John 19:30 KJV). With one last surge of strength, He pressed His torn feet against the nail, took a deep breath, and uttered, *"Father, into thy hands I commend my spirit"* (Luke 23:46 KJV). With that, Jesus hung His head and died. A Roman soldier walked over to confirm his death by piercing Jesus in the side, which caused a sudden flow of blood and water. Sadly, Jesus was already dead. [12]

---

[12] Information derived from Matthew 27, Mark 15, Luke 23, John 19, and Internet research "A Physician Testifies About the Crucifixion," Dr. C. Truman Davis, New Wine Magazine, April, 1982.

What was Jesus' storm? Why did He have to die such a painful death? What did He do wrong? NOTHING! He was perfect. His death on the cross was so that we might have a right to eternal life and that, ultimately, the Father would be glorified.

If you compare the death that Jesus experienced on the cross to the storms that we face and the sacrifices God requires of us, you quickly recognize that our experiences pale in comparison.

All for His Glory

The scriptures are full of passages that indicate that our purpose is to glorify God. When you think about this from our limited human perspective, it appears very selfish of God to create something just to give Him glory. But 1 Corinthians 10:26 declares, "*The earth is the Lord's, and everything in it.*" Contrary to what we sometimes think with our independent attitudes, we belong to God, and all that we do should benefit Him. 1 Corinthians 10:31 tells us, "*So whether you eat or drink or whatever you do, do it all for the glory of God.*" There is no question that our lives should exemplify Christ so that God gets the glory: "*But grow in the grace and knowledge of our Lord and Savior Jesus Christ. To him be glory both now and forever! Amen*" (2 Peter 3:18).

There is a popular cliché in the Christian community that "salvation is free." We must be careful giving the world the impression that it costs nothing – salvation costs your life.

Luke 9:23-25 declares: "*If anyone would come after me, he must deny himself and take up his cross daily and follow me. For whoever wants to save his life will lose it, but whoever loses his life for me will save it. What good is it for a man to gain the whole world and yet lose or forfeit his very self?*"

Following Christ costs you everything, but the reward system is awesome. A bonus system at your job, a pension your employer provides, or even a raise for your performance does not compare to God's reward system for those who seek His will. Psalm 119:1-2 states, *"Blessed are they whose ways are blameless, who walk according to the law of the Lord. Blessed are they who keep his statutes and seek him with all their heart."*

The Lord desires to shower us with blessings, but the shower has a prerequisite; we must be obedient to His Word. In Deuteronomy 28:1-2, Moses told the Israelites about the favor of God and what they needed to do to receive that favor: *"If you fully obey the Lord your God and carefully follow all his commands I give you today, the Lord your God will set you high above all the nations on earth. All these blessings will come upon you and accompany you if you obey the Lord your God."*

There is a reward when it is all for His glory! There are blessings behind the storm when it is all for His glory! There is growth for you when it is all for His glory! No matter how difficult the process seems, in the end, you will know that the storm was **FOR YOUR GOOD AND FOR HIS GLORY!**

> <u>**Encouragement For Those in the Storm:**</u> For those who are still in their storm, I leave you these words from Numbers 6:24 – *The Lord bless you, and keep you; the Lord make His face shine upon you, and be gracious to you; the Lord turn his face toward you, and give you peace.* He will keep you through the storm. Using the motto of Alcoholics Anonymous: One Day at a Time®, you can make it through your storm.

Bonus Chapters

Chapter 11

Illness Can Take You by Storm

As I reread and edited this 20-year-old testimony, I can easily see how the storms in my life were for my good and for His glory. I can honestly say that despite the rough days, weeks, months, and years, I don't think I would tap out of those storms today if I could turn back the hands of time. I love the person I am today, and it's because of how those storms molded and shaped me. They also prepared me for the many more storms to come.

When you look back on storms, you gain incredible insight. Those storms I shared in the original book release were for that season. As I grew in Christ, the devil realized the storms that used to knock me on my heels now barely caused a shake. I learned how to deal with the storm caused by outside forces attacking my family or me – that is the enemy I can see. I learned from my storm of disobedience that I was in control of whether that type of storm would reappear. The easy answer is to be obedient.

The next two decades would be filled with storms that attacked my heart and were aimed at destabilizing my emotions. The emotional toll had an impact on everything else in life. When your heart is aching, it's hard to focus on what you need to give your full attention. Everything begins to blend. The first is the storm of illness. Whether it is your illness or the illness of a family member, it is a heart-wrenching experience. What do you do when your body is attacked with illness, and there's nothing you can do to cure it? What happens when illness hits your family – your children, grandchildren, parents, or siblings?

Sickness and Pain

Let's revisit Job. After the Lord allows satan to strip Job of his livestock, kill his servants, and kill his children, his brother, and his brother's family, he then allows satan to take his health. "**So [s]atan went out from the presence of the Lord and afflicted Job with painful sores from the soles of his feet to the crown of his head**" (Job 2:7). In response to Job's wife's frustration with his faithfulness to God after all that happened, Job responds, "**...Shall we accept good from God, and not trouble?**" (Job 2:10). Job had a level of commitment that takes years of growth. Job not only had painful sores, but they also had to be unsightly. I can only imagine how the sores must have looked after he scraped them with the piece of broken pottery as described in Job 2:8. I have never been that sick, but putting myself in Job's shoes, my heart aches for him.

Let's not gloss over the rest of the book of Job because, in the next chapter, Job's humanity shows itself. The chapter begins with Job cursing the day of his birth. In responding to his not-so-supportive friends, he declares in Job 6:8-9, "**Oh, that I might have my request, that God would grant what I hope for, that God would be willing to crush me, to let loose his hand and cut off my life!**" This statement is more of what I expected, given all that Job has been through. Job finally pours out the anguish inside of him. What I like about the next several scenes where Job is debating with his "friends" is that he is aware that God can hear everything he is saying. He is expressing his feelings to the Father while arguing with his friends. What's important to know is that

God can take it. Sometimes we have to say aloud to God what's in our heart, even when it doesn't have all the religious platitudes.

Before we leave Job, let me say that your support system matters when you're in the storm. Eliphaz, Bildad, and Zophar blamed Job for his troubles. They had no idea what was happening in the background, but that's beside the point. Job did not need his friends to come in and point fingers at him. In Job 16:2, after hearing his friends droll on and on, he says, "**I have heard many things like these; you are miserable comforters, all of you! Will your long-winded speeches never end?**" In chapter 19, he asks Bildad, "**How long will you torment me and crush me with your words?**" Job needed empathy, consolation, and support - not lectures. These were the wrong people for Job because they did not provide what he needed. You must make sure you have the right people in your tribe. Your tribe can be friends, family, or both, but you need people who are in it with you until the end. I heard someone say once, "You can be sick, but don't be sick too long." Your tribe must be there for the long haul of the illness, not just until they get too busy, lose patience, or simply become uninvested in you. You may need to remove some people from your tribe if they are doing more harm than good, and you might have to add some people to your tribe whom you didn't expect but God sent.

If you are part of someone's tribe, be diligent and faithful in your support. No matter how long the illness lasts, you cannot check out because the clock in your head says, "I've been supportive long enough." If God has assigned you to be there for someone in their illness, don't mess up the assignment, and don't decide to ignore it because, as I discovered, disobedience can land you in the belly.

Standing on the Sidelines

There is a level of helplessness that is paralyzing when someone around you is ill, but when it's your child or grandchild, it's a gut punch. In some ways, this storm is more difficult because you cannot fight the battle on their behalf. You can't remove their pain, and you can't heal them. I've experienced three health-related storms with my children and one with my father. In the cases of my children, they were grown and living on their own. However, anyone who is a parent (by birth or by gift) knows that age doesn't matter when it comes to protecting your children.

The first experience was with a daughter. My husband was in the process of opening Open the Book Ministries, a church plant, and the same week of the launch, we were sitting in Fairfax County Hospital as a surgeon cut open our daughter's head to remove a brain tumor. She was only 26 years old, a homeowner in the prime of her life, and progressing in her career. This diagnosis was not supposed to be the next step in her journey, but a storm hits when you least expect it and derails your plans. We were trying to focus on establishing a new ministry while churning inside about our child's life-threatening illness. This storm was one of the scariest of my life. You deal with the "what-ifs" and worry about the worst case.

As we sat in the waiting room, we had no other options – all we could do was pray. The prognosis was not good when the doctor came out sooner than expected – the tumor was cancerous. Our 26-year-old daughter had an inoperable cancerous brain tumor. We were unprepared for that prognosis as the storm shifted from a Category 3 to a Category 5 hurricane. We were not ready for that news. You've been there when you get news that knocks the wind out of you.

The next four months were filled with chemo, radiation, spinal tap, bone marrow, steroids, and more. This storm of illness continued to strengthen, and there was nothing we could do. We did all we could to support her, including moving her back home. The storm required her to be dependent on her parents, and it required us to support her emotionally, mentally, and physically. That's what we do for our children and those we love.

The emotional toll it took on her and us cannot be described. Watching your child in pain and feeling completely helpless ranks at the top of the charts for the worst feelings in the world. There was one instance where she was in so much pain that she needed to go to the hospital. I could not help her down the stairs to the car because touching her anywhere sent pain through her body. I felt such helplessness! The ambulance came and took her to the emergency room, and as she lay in the room to be examined, I stood outside the room, still feeling helpless. I wanted to fix it and make her better, but like Job, her healing was in God's hands. Here is where standing on the Word of God becomes essential. The Psalmist understood this when he said, "*From the end of the earth will I cry unto thee, when my heart is overwhelmed: lead me to the rock that is higher than I*" (Psalm 61:2b). You go to the ROCK when there is no place else to turn.

It's easy to become angry with God when you or a loved one is ill. "Why me?" you may ask. This is a persistent and nagging question. A friend once replied to me, "Why not you?" Mother Teresa had the right perspective when she said, "I know God will not give me anything I can't handle; I just wish He didn't trust me so much."[13] The idea that our storm is God trusting us with the circumstances is deep. The storm isn't always only about us. Indeed, we often go through storms that will help someone else. God may be trusting you to push through this storm so He can use you to help someone.

---

[13] https://andiquote.org/quote/1629/

The second storm was my son's. In this case, he was not ill, but his youngest daughter was. At two years old, she developed double pneumonia and was hospitalized. You want to protect your children from all pain, but Jesus' words in John 16:33 apply to them, "*In this world, you will have trouble.*" As my son and his wife rearranged their lives and that of their two older children, they faced a storm out of their control. The doctors were running tests on my granddaughter, trying to nail down the cause of the illness. In the meantime, her parents were exhausted and battling emotions of fear and anxiety. The entire family was praying. The pain of watching your granddaughter lay in a hospital bed coughing until it hurt with tubes and machines connected to her body and her parents trying their best to hold it together was a feeling of paralyzing helplessness. Thankfully, I was not traveling for work, and I was able to help with the other kids, but I could not make my granddaughter better or relieve her parent's anguish.

It's hard to understand the purpose of a child being ill. As a mature Christian, you try to understand the why. I read a quote that I cannot remember who authored, but it challenges: if God never tells you why, will you still trust Him? The reality is: bad things happen to good people, and we must trust God even when we don't understand. David understood the human psyche when he admonished, "*Trust in the Lord with all your heart and lean not on your own understanding; in all your ways submit to him, and he will make your paths straight*" (Proverbs 3:5-6). God won't always explain. When He feels distant, that is when we need to trust more.

The third experience I'll share is about another daughter who was scheduled for a routine procedure. She was expected to be home the same day or the next day after the procedure, but there's always that small percentage risk of things going wrong. That happened in her case. Her short hospital stay turned into a week and included a second unexpected surgery and some scary moments of concern by the doctors. I had just had foot surgery and was recovering in another state, so I could not travel to help her.

While I was right there by the side of my first daughter when she was ill, I could not be with the second one. I could only talk to her on the phone when she felt well enough, which would be for short periods because of pain meds and the constant flow of medical personnel. I could only get updates secondhand from family visiting the hospital, so I had to depend on someone else to keep me informed. In addition, COVID-19 restrictions were still in effect and created visitation barriers. I ran smack into the control issues I worked so hard to release. I had no control over this situation or my ability to travel to get to her, and I wasn't even able to devise a way to "pretend" control. It was all in God's hands.

The reality is that each of these situations was in God's hands, but in our humanity, we try to think we can help God be God. He never has and never will need our help, but we often want to intervene because we think we know what's best. God will bring us to where it becomes crystal clear that there is no other way but His. Our way is worry and anguish; His way is faith and trust.

Worry: this is something we have difficulty controlling. In the Christian community, you hear statements like, "If you're going to pray, don't worry, and if you're going to worry, don't pray." Like many Christian colloquialisms, this sounds good, but it isn't easy to implement. One of my favorite passages of scripture is Philippians 4: 6-7, "***Do not be anxious about anything, but in every situation, by prayer and petition, with thanksgiving, present your requests to God. And the peace of God, which transcends all understanding, will guard your hearts and our minds in Christ Jesus.***" This is a promise from God that we can claim amid the storm of sickness. He promises to give us peace that transcends all understanding that will guard our hearts and minds, but there are four conditions for that peace:

1. Don't be anxious.
2. Pray and petition.
3. Present your requests.
4. Give thanks.

By mastering these four things, we gain His peace. But how do we keep that peace? We may find that peace for a day or a week, but worry has a way of creeping back in. In Philippians 4:8, Paul prescribes how we can keep worry at bay, "***Finally, brothers and sisters, whatever is true, whatever is noble, whatever is right, whatever is pure, whatever is lovely, whatever is admirable – if anything is excellent or praiseworthy – think about such things.***" Paul advises us to keep our minds preoccupied with pleasant things so we are not overshadowed by worry.

It is by no means easy to train the mind not to worry. Still, Paul encourages us in 1 Corinthians 10:5, "***we demolish arguments and every pretension that sets itself up against the knowledge of God, and we take captive every thought to make it obedient to Christ.***" Worry is one of those arguments that sets itself up against the knowledge of Christ, so we must take it captive consciously. When illness impacts your life, you must fight the devil's attacks on your mind by being deliberate about what you allow to occupy your mind.

Think on these things!

Chapter 12

Loss and Grief – The Longest Storm Ever

For most of my childhood and adulthood, loss and grief were not an experience that hit close to home. Aunts, uncles, and cousins passed away, and I felt a sense of sadness and loss, but I had not experienced the gut punch type of loss. It was the kind of loss where the ugly cry didn't last too long. They were losses where I could remember fond memories and smile without that pain in my heart. That all began to change in 2014.

The illnesses I described in the previous chapter had happy endings: my family members were healed. However, the last decade has been filled with sickness that ended in death, and the loss and associated grief seem like the longest storm ever. In the ten years between 2012 and 2022, I experienced the deaths of my mother-in-law, father-in-law, sister-in-law, brother-in-law, three uncles, an aunt, two friends, several cousins, my second father, and my dad. Those losses were not equal, and each impacted my heart and emotions differently. I would need to write another book to share how each person impacted me and why their deaths were a storm for me, so I will not share about all of them at this time.

In 2014 and 2015, two friends passed away within a year of each other. They were both trustees in our church, and they were longtime friends. In the first case, my friend had been ill for several weeks but seemed to be getting better. We believed God would heal her. She took a turn for the worst, and we got the call to come to the hospital when she was placed on a ventilator. My husband and I were in the waiting room with family and friends as her loved ones went in to say farewell before she was removed from the ventilator. She was 46 years young and left to mourn a husband and four grown children. With the second friend, he was waiting to be released from the hospital after a surgical procedure. As he and his wife waited for the doctor to sign off on the release, he got up to use the restroom, said he was not feeling well, and went into cardiac arrest. As his wife looked on in complete shock, the hospital staff tried to revive his heart, but he was pronounced dead. He was 53 years old and left to mourn a wife and three grown children.

These were friends, and they departed this earth relatively young. They didn't get to retire and collect their pensions. They didn't get to see their grandchildren grow up. They didn't get to move to their retirement location with their spouses and live out their golden years. They left a hole in our hearts that could never be replaced. We mourned as a church for what seemed like forever. We lost one leader and a beautiful soul in August 2014; before we could recover from that, we lost another in 2015. For me, it was a gut punch and a reality check. I remember crying several times, but shock and disbelief paralyzed me.

We have all heard that there are five stages of grief: denial, anger, bargaining, depression, and acceptance. We may not experience all five and don't always experience them in this order. In both cases, I was stuck in denial for a long time. I could not believe they were both gone – it seemed impossible. She was younger than me, and he was about the same age. How could they be gone?

In both cases, the surviving spouse did not handle the details of the finances. Therefore, I helped the spouses work through the financial responsibilities they were left with. Proverbs 18:16 tells us that a man's gift will make room for him. Despite any grief I felt, I suppressed it to help this widow and widower who were now experiencing life without their companions.

> *"Praise be to the God and Father of our Lord Jesus Christ, the Father of compassion and the God of all comfort, who comforts us in all our troubles, so that we can comfort those in any trouble with the comfort we ourselves receive from God."* – 2 Corinthians 1:3-4

What I learned through the death of my friends was that life is short and tomorrow is not promised. Take advantage of every opportunity to live, laugh, and love. When I think of "her," I smile because I remember her infectious smile, but I also ache for her husband because he wakes up every day without her. When I think of "him," I can't help but appreciate what a provider and protector he was of his wife. His death was hard to accept because it was sudden and unexpected; he was about to walk out of the hospital. The gnawing "why" question surrounds death as it does illness, but the reality is that God does not always explain. *"Our God is in heaven; he does whatever pleases him."* (Psalm 115:3). This includes calling him home. He reminds me every time I think of him that tomorrow is not promised to us, but neither is the next hour. I think about his wife and the rebuilding process I watched her go through as she adjusted to this new normal.

Both friends' deaths were a gut punch and a wake-up call for me. I've learned to *"Be very careful, then, how you live – not as unwise, but as wise"* (Ephesians 5:15). I am mindful of David's prayer in Psalm 90:12, *"Teach us to number our days, that we may gain a heart of wisdom."* I don't remember my last conversation with either friend, but it might be different if I knew it was my last. Wisdom says to learn from experience and handle each conversation as if it could be your last.

THE STORM: FOR YOUR GOOD AND FOR HIS GLORY

The death of my aunt rocked me to the core. I'd lost my maternal grandparents before writing this book's first edition. Their deaths were nine months apart. They were my first experiences with the death of someone close to me. I remember burying myself in my work after my grandmother's death, which may not be the ideal way to process the loss of a loved one if it means suppressing the grief. However, it was the death of Auntie that pierced my heart. She was Auntie Louise, my father's older sister, who owned the house where we grew up. To myself and my siblings, she was just "Auntie." She lived on the second floor, and we lived on the first floor all our childhood and part of my teen years. She was not just an aunt but a second mother and the stand-in for my paternal grandmother. My paternal grandmother died when my dad was 15, and his sister stepped in to help their grieving father take care of my dad and his younger sister. Auntie was a staple in my life; she was there for every major event: high school graduation, college graduation, and wedding. Auntie was that person I could always count on being in my corner. Although she lived to 92, that didn't decrease my pain from her loss. It's been eight years since she passed, and I still miss her like it was yesterday.

Momentous events happen during life, and you remember where you were and what you were doing when they happened. I remember all the details surrounding receiving the news. I got home late from a work event, and my husband told me she was gone. I remember hearing the news and not knowing what to do besides cry the "ugly cry." It wasn't a surprise; she was in the hospital, and I had spoken to her the previous day on the phone and just prayed because she couldn't speak much. I knew she would not leave the hospital, and that could be my last conversation with her. But grief doesn't always make sense. There are no rules with grief. I cried as if I didn't know she was very ill. I had to lie down because I felt faint. The physical anguish was my first experience with the storm side of loss. This wasn't a rainstorm; it was a full-on tornado. I experienced more stages of grief after Auntie's death, but still not all. I remember being in denial and having a bit of depression before I moved to acceptance.

I knew my life would be forever different without Auntie. As I write this with tears in my eyes, I'm reminded that grief can be the longest storm ever. It doesn't go away; it just changes. While I am no longer overwhelmed emotionally by the thought of the loss, not a family event goes by where I don't think of her and get teary. My family members still talk about her constantly. I still miss her, but I'm glad she is no longer here dealing with illness.

It's hard not to tell the story of every loved one, but I'll stick to my promise. But I must mention my Uncle Sammy's death which came a year after his sister's. It was significant because it meant that out of my father's family of 13, there were only three remaining: #11, #12, and #13. He was the only brother my dad had remaining in Boston and was his hanging partner. This event elevated the notion that grieving is personal and transferrable. I was going to miss my uncle, but it was overshadowed by the fact that my dad would miss him even more.

> *"Carry each other's burdens, and in this way you fulfill the law of Christ." – Galatians 6:2*

My forever Pastor and father-in-law was a monumental loss because he was bigger than life and positively influenced the lives of so many. His loss was also heartbreaking for me because it was the first time I sat and watched someone die. I remember everything about that afternoon. His health declined rapidly over a few weeks, and after being shifted to hospice care, we waited for the call to come. For days, the family sat bedside, ensuring he was comfortable, and when God was ready to take him home, we were gathered around his bed. His eldest son prayed as he took his last breaths, and the Amen of the prayer matched the last breath. It was sad and beautiful at the same time. The most difficult thing was mourning the loss of the man who was my

Pastor from age six and became my father-in-law while at the same time trying to support my husband as best as possible. My husband was a daddy's boy, and this giant of a man supported him and helped him become the person he is now. My husband is not like me; losing it emotionally without warning, but the loss impacted him deeply.

Others expected more emotion from my husband. He preached his dad's eulogy, and one might not have known the depth of their relationship by his composure. He was honoring his dad with his message – it was part of his grieving process.

We all grieve differently – it's a personal thing. We must allow people to grieve their way and support them in their grief. Grieving is impacted by who we are, our relationship with the deceased, and our stage in the grieving process. It is important to note that grieving doesn't always begin at death. As someone's health fails, we may start grieving before death. I'll talk more about that shortly.

After my father-in-law's death, there seemed to be a flurry of losses back-to-back. My Uncle Jeep passed away four months later (he was best friends with my father-in-law), and three months after that, my Uncle Tommy died. Neither was a surprise as they were both ill, but let me help some of you who are supporting others – the fact that the person who passed away was a senior or sick does not make the grieving process easier. People say, "Well, they lived a good long life." How is that helpful to my grief? It's not! Grief says, "I want them to live forever, so I don't have to feel this pain."

Uncle Tommy's death was difficult for many reasons. The memories of Uncle Tommy driving from North Carolina to our house in Boston and ringing the doorbell at 2 or 3 am until someone answered are forever etched in my mind. He was THAT uncle.

Uncle Tommy and my dad were like twins born 15 months apart. My sister gave them the nickname "bookends." There was something connected about them; even their illnesses were the same: neck surgery, prostate cancer, stroke, heart disease, and kidney disease. We knew that his brother's death would be hard on Dad. When Uncle Tommy's health declined and he passed away, my dad had COVID, so no one could visit him to tell him in person. We had to keep his brother's death from him for two weeks until he was well enough to receive a socially distanced visit. As a family, we agreed to have the Chaplain tell him in the morning, and my mom and sister arrived in the afternoon to help him process the news. His reaction was the grief one would expect from losing a twin. Our family surrounded Dad with love as he processed the death of his brother through the visits allowed in the lobby, phone calls and Zoom calls. The loss of my uncle was tough because he was so close to my dad. If you saw one of them at any family gathering, you saw the other. So, knowing Dad was hurting from the pain of grief was difficult.

One of the reasons I feel that grief and loss can be the longest storms ever is that you never get over the fact that you won't see that loved one again on this side of heaven. You never stop missing that person; you only learn to cope.

Again, it's hard for me not to tell the story of every loved one I've lost, but maybe someday I will write that book on grief and share how each person impacted me and why their deaths were a storm for me.

Life Will Never Be the Same

I count myself blessed. God allowed me to have my parents on this earth until my mid-50s. I know so many people who were not as fortunate. And yet, losing my dad didn't feel easier because I was older and had been blessed to have him for so long. Again, grief doesn't have rules to follow. The loss of my dad changed my life. The pain didn't feel any lighter despite starting my grieving process before he died.

In 2018, my dad had a major stroke in North Carolina while attending my Uncle Tommy's vow renewal ceremony, and my dad was set to be the best man. He went to the barbershop with his brother for a haircut, and I got a call while at breakfast from Uncle Tommy saying that he could not move his legs. My sisters and I rushed to the barbershop and took him to the hospital. The Emergency Department (ED) doctors declared Dad did not have a stroke. They were not sure what was happening but wanted to run tests. Dad's speech was a little slurred, but he got movement back in his legs, so I told my sisters, Mom, and the rest of the family to go to the ceremony, and I would stay with Dad until they released him. In my head, we'd be at the church before the ceremony was over. We were in the ED for quite a few hours, waiting for an MRI to be done. It was a weekend, so things were running slower than normal. As hours passed in the ED, Dad got worse. I remember texting my husband while he was at the ceremony and telling him to return to the hospital because something was wrong. I didn't know what was happening, but I knew my dad was not okay. The neurologist arrived and said my dad had a Transient Ischemic Attack (TIA), a brief stroke-like attack. They decided to hold him for a few days to run more tests.

They eventually moved him to a room on an internal medicine floor (not a neurological unit) and said a doctor would come to see him. I remember telling the hospital personnel that something was wrong – they kept telling me the doctor was on rounds and would be by to see him. Because I had no medical degree, there was nothing I could do. I could only watch him get worse right in the hospital. According to their paperwork, he did not have a stroke, so the nurses did not see his progressing symptoms as needing immediate attention.

Sitting in the hospital with my dad and my husband, waiting for the doctor to come by and for my family to come from the ceremony, I prayed that God would intervene. I prayed that my dad would not continue to get worse. This wasn't my illness, but I was 100% feeling the impact of this storm. But God doesn't always answer how and when we want him. My anxiety was through the roof as I watched the strongest man I knew decline. My dad survived a triple bypass, prostate cancer, and back surgery; I couldn't accept what my eyes were seeing. This storm was the storm of illness I described in the previous chapter.

That doctor showed up hours later after the stroke damaged his body. Without describing all the details of his decline that day (which are painful), I can tell you that his speech was impaired by the end of the day, and his right side was paralyzed. As I previously mentioned about my children's illnesses, that feeling of helplessness took over. For a long time after this, I had Post Traumatic Stress Disorder (PTSD). Anytime I heard the word stroke, I would become anxious and stressed. I kept asking myself: what could I have done differently? It took some time before I could answer - nothing.

The reality is that sometimes God's will is not pretty. That sounds contrary to what we believe should happen. We expect rainbows and sunshine, but that doesn't align with scripture. The Bible has stories of many whose experiences didn't align with rainbows and sunshine. We've explored Job extensively, but there's Paul, who spent several years in prison for the sake of Christ (Acts 16 and 21), David, who King Saul wanted to kill because of jealousy (1 Samuel 19), and Jesus, who was crucified for being the Son of God (Matthew 27). It is about bringing God glory.

The entire family came to the hospital after the ceremony, and prayers surrounded the room. While my dad lay in the hospital with his health deteriorating by the hour, he made a confession of faith and gave his life to Jesus. This son of a preacher who spent all his childhood in church surrendered his heart to God. As my husband led him to accept Christ as his personal Savior and Lord, he commented, "I should have done this a long time ago."

After the stroke, my dad spent over three years in a long-term care hospital. He got his speech back but never walked again, and his right side was severely compromised. Despite his disabilities, my dad continued to enjoy life. We became closer as a family because we had a common goal of caring for Dad. Romans 8:28 was fulfilled, "*For we know, all things work together for the good to them that love God, to them who are called according to His purpose.*"

In 2020, COVID-19 was in full swing and running rampant throughout senior living facilities. The facilities were locked down, and we could only communicate with him via telephone and a weekly Zoom call. Despite our prayers, my dad caught COVID and was moved from his floor into a COVID unit. All we could do was call him on the phone and pray. We prayed continuously because so many people had died and were dying from COVID, and we were worried because Dad was at high risk at 86 years old with heart and kidney disease. I remember being in the garage painting cabinet doors and the scripture from John 11:4 came to me, "*This sickness will not end in death. No, it is for God's glory so that God's Son may be glorified through it.*"

And that scripture was fulfilled. My dad "kicked COVID's butt." After three weeks in the COVID unit, Dad returned to his room. His roommate also caught COVID, but the impact of the disease on his body was more damaging, and he lost his battle. My dad finally got to see his family in person when the facility reopened a year later, but not his bookend brother, who passed away. We were blessed to spend time with him and had an 87th birthday celebration for him in person (his 86th was a drive-by party). Then his health started to deteriorate.

We noticed small signs of Dad's decline starting in August 2021. By October, it was clear to us that things were shifting. I remember thinking on my birthday in November that this would be my last birthday with my dad alive. Because I was living in another state, I relied on my siblings for health updates on my dad. My sister was talking with the medical team, who also noticed a decline. I established a nightly routine with my dad after he recovered from COVID. I would call him between 7:30 pm and 8:30 pm every night before he went to bed, and we'd talk about random things. He always asked what I did that day and if I exercised. The nightly calls are one of the things I miss most. Whether we talked for 45 minutes or 10 minutes, it was all good for me. While I never say the stroke was a good thing, it did work out for our good because we strengthened our relationship on our nightly calls. Once again, Romans 8:28 was being fulfilled.

Soon COVID reared its ugly head again, and the facility was closed to visitors just before Christmas 2021. We knew Dad would not survive the isolation again if they were closed too long. He made it through over a year of quarantine in 2020 but wouldn't survive another one like that. Between December 2021 and January 2022, things declined rapidly. Dad's kidneys were failing, and dialysis was not an option we would choose for him.

Here is where the grieving started. The preparation for someone's death is the beginning of grieving. The first stage of grief, denial, can start here. It's also when we start bargaining for more time or a change in the diagnosis. With my dad, I was torn between: I don't want him to suffer, and I don't want to let him go.

I knew it was his time, but I was having trouble accepting the reality that soon, my dad would be gone. There would be a day that I could not call him to say goodnight. I increased my visits to Boston to spend as much time with him as possible. In January, he was placed on hospice care and allowed compassionate care visits from visitors for one hour three times a week. I flew into

Boston to see him for my visit on January 17th, MLK Jr.'s birthday. Because he had visitors on Friday, Saturday, and Sunday, the facility said he was out of visits until Friday. I was fully prepared to storm the door and make a run for his room, but my sister got him moved to end-of-life visits which allowed visitors daily. At this point, doctors predicted he had 10-14 days to live.

I remember my last in-person visit with Dad like it was yesterday. As with all my visits, I never told him I was coming – with the flight issues, I never wanted him to be disappointed. He was surprised as always, and even though he could not get out of bed, it was great to see his handsome face. We talked about random things, like usual. I thanked him for teaching me the value of hard work. I told him I watched how he went to work every day, no matter what. Even after the blizzard of '78, as soon as the main road was plowed, Dad trekked through 27" of snow to get to work. I thanked him for teaching us respect for elders, and I thanked him for my first name-brand Jordache jeans, which was a big deal for a 15-year-old in the 80s. I wanted to stay longer, but I didn't want to violate the hour limit and jeopardize future visits, so I told him I had to go, but I'd be back soon. As he lay in the bed smiling, I laid my head on his chest as if I knew it was the last time I'd see him on this side of heaven. I already had my flight to come back, but I knew that tomorrow was not promised. I told him I loved him and tried not to cry because I knew he'd tell me to stop crying.

I returned on January 21st to visit Dad with my mother for our scheduled visit the next day. My sister Renee and our cousin visited the day before, and Renee said Dad was in pain. His kidneys were shutting down and sending toxins through his body. She said the doctor provided pain medication, and Dad was resting peacefully when she left. My mother and I arrived just before 1pm while the residents were at lunch. Dad's nurse's assistant came out as we were waiting to put on protective equipment and let us know she said had just been to see him, and he was resting. She told him that his daughter would be here soon. After being suited up, my mom and I went to his room, and he was resting peacefully. I sat on the bed and let him know we were there. I held his hand and started talking to him quietly. After a few minutes, I looked at his chest and noticed it was not moving. I told my mother, "I don't think he's breathing." She asked if I felt a pulse; I checked but could not get a pulse. I said, "I think he's gone." I went to get the nurse's assistant and told her I thought my dad was gone. I knew the answer already, but the denial stage of grief was already beginning.

On January 22nd at 1:15 pm, my dad was gone. I could only call my siblings and say, "he's gone." The toughest man I knew was gone. A part of me was so grateful at how peaceful he looked lying there – so peaceful that I thought he was sleeping. But my chest ached, which reminded me that no matter how much at peace he was, I was in pain.

For a while, I kept telling myself that if we'd come earlier, I could have seen him one more time. If I had arrived at 12:30pm, I could have been here, so he wasn't alone when he passed. He didn't wait for me to come. One day my sister Renee said to me, "If you were meant to be there, you would have been. He wouldn't have wanted you there." That was so true, the nurse's assistant told him that his daughter was arriving soon, but he didn't wait.

I attended grief classes, and in the first class, they emphasized Hebrews 9:27, "***And as it is appointed for men to die once, but after this the judgment*** (KJV)." My dad had an appointment. Somewhere between 1:00 pm and 1:15 pm on January 22nd, God called for him to come home. That may not have been the time I would have chosen, but the thing about God is that His will won't always align with ours.

> ***"For My thoughts are not your thoughts, neither are your ways My ways,"*** *declares the Lord.* ***"As the heavens are higher than the earth, so are My ways***

higher than your ways and My thoughts than your thoughts. *"* (Isaiah 55:8-9)

The death of a parent is different. I've never experienced the death of a child, which I imagine is the definition of the longest storm ever. The death of my dad became about legacy for me. I had the opportunity to meet Earvin "Magic" Johnson at a work conference for my current employer that took place the week after my dad's funeral. When celebrity guests speak at our conferences, the company assigns a staff person to host them. I was Magic's host. When I met him at the elevators and walked toward his meet and greet room, he asked, "How are you doing? How's your family?" I replied that my dad had passed last month, and we were dealing with the loss. He responded with something that has become my motivation. He said, "You are his legacy."

I am my dad's legacy. He and my mom have deposited traits in me that I must use to help others and change the world. I will always grieve the loss of my Dad. Some days the grief ambush hits hard, and it takes more than a minute to recover. On other days, I'm fully on my game, reminding myself that I AM HIS LEGACY. I have this on my bedroom wall framed and surrounded by pictures of my dad and me. My siblings and I are what the world will know of my dad going forward. He wasn't famous and won't be in any history books, but we will remember him as the man who produced five amazing people who are making their mark on the world.

My grief story is not your story. Every story is different. I can say for me going to GriefShare© at my church was helpful. The materials helped me to understand what I was feeling and manage myself. That may not work for you but find what does. For some of us, it's not enough to quote Psalm 30:5, "***For his anger endureth but a moment; in his favour is life: weeping may endure for a night, but joy cometh in the morning*** (KJV)." The morning isn't necessarily tomorrow morning.

Even if you reach the acceptance stage of grief, that does not mean it's over; it just means it's different. That's why grief and loss is the longest storm ever. You'll always miss that loved one. The storm's winds may have subsided, and the rain may have dried up, but the damage to your heart from the loss will always be present. You will battle grief ambush. Grief ambush is when something unexpected triggers you, with no advance notice, to experience that deep sense of loss you thought you'd move past. But remember, your storm isn't always only about you. There may be someone you are supposed to use your grief story to help. As hard as it was to pen the words of my story, I'm sure it helped someone. Someone is dealing with a loss similar to yours, and you may be able to encourage them - sometimes, we all need someone who will listen.

It will be one year from the day my dad got his wings when this book is released. I think about him every day - some days, it is great memories, and other days it's the ache of the loss. But because my dad accepted Christ as his personal Savior and Lord, I grieve with hope.

> *"Brothers and sisters, we do not want you to be uninformed about those who sleep in death, so that you do not grieve like the rest of mankind, who have no hope. For we believe that Jesus died and rose again, and so we believe that God will bring with Jesus those who have fallen asleep in him. According to the Lord's word, we tell you that we who are still alive, who are left until the coming of the Lord, will certainly not precede those who have fallen asleep. For the Lord himself will come down from heaven, with a loud command, with the voice of the archangel and with the trumpet call of God, and the dead in Christ will rise first. 17 After that, we who are still alive and are left will be caught up together with them in the clouds to meet the Lord in the air. And so we will be with the Lord forever. 18 Therefore*

> *encourage one another with these words."* (1 Thessalonians 4:13-18)

Every day, I'm grateful that I was blessed to have him as my dad, and I'm reminded:

> *"Rejoice always, pray continually, give thanks in all circumstances; for this is God's will for you in Christ Jesus."* (1 Thessalonians 5:16-18)

I will see him again.

Encouragement for Your Storm

Since relocating to Florida, I've noticed that the sky changes very quickly when a storm approaches. The darker the sky, the stronger the storm. Some storms require storm prep because of the expected damage. When you root yourself in the Word of God - that's storm prep. When you make sure your prayer life is consistent and not just a blessing over the food - that's storm prep. When you work on having a relationship with the Father daily, and not just when you need something - that's storm prep. Storms are inevitable, so storm prep is critical. Whatever storm is in front of you, around you, or moving into your rear mirror, the answer is always to remain anchored. The purpose of anchoring a boat is so that it is not pulled out to sea by the winds and the waves. We need to throw down our anchor before the storm arrives to weather the storm.

I leave you with the words of the song by the late Douglas Miller, released in 1985, that remain as powerful today.

> "Though the storms keep on raging in my life
> And sometimes it's hard to tell
> the night from day
> Still, that hope that lies within is reassured
> As I keep my eyes upon the distant shore
> I know He'll lead me safely to that blessed place He has prepared
> But if the storms don't cease
> And if the winds keep on blowing
> My soul has been anchored in the Lord
> Oh, I realize that sometimes in this life,
> we're gonna be tossed
> By the waves and the currents that seem so fierce
> But in the Word of God, I've got an anchor
> And it keeps me steadfast and unmovable
> despite the tides
> But if the storms don't cease
> And just in case the winds,
> they keep on blowing in my life
> My soul has been anchored in, in the Lord."

From one storm survivor to another, be anchored!

www.ingramcontent.com/pod-product-compliance
Lightning Source LLC
Chambersburg PA
CBHW060833050426
42453CB00008B/677